W.

The Balance of Power Between Russia and NATO in the Arctic and High North

Sidharth Kaushal, James Byrne, Joseph Byrne, Giangiuseppe Pili and Gary Somerville

www.rusi.org

Royal United Services Institute for Defence and Security Studies

The Balance of Power Between Russia and NATO in the Arctic and High North
First published 2022

Whitehall Papers series

Series Editor: Professor Malcolm Chalmers
Editor: Dr Emma De Angelis

RUSI is a Registered Charity (No. 210639)
Paperback ISBN [978-1-032-30965-1] eBook ISBN [978-1-003-30839-3]
Published on behalf of the Royal United Services Institute for Defence and Security Studies
by
Routledge Journals, an imprint of Taylor & Francis, 4 Park Square, Milton Park, Abingdon OX14 4RN

Image Credit: The Project 885 Yasen class Kazan nuclear submarine arrives at its permanent deployment base of the Russian Navy Northern Fleet in Severomorsk on Russia's Arctic coast. *Courtesy of Lev Fedoseyev/TASS/Alamy Live News*

SUBSCRIPTIONS
Please send subscription order to:

USA/Canada: Taylor & Francis Inc., Journals Department, 325 Chestnut Street, 8th Floor, Philadelphia, PA 19106 USA

UK/Rest of World: Routledge Journals, T&F Customer Services, T&F Informa UK Ltd, Sheepen Place, Colchester, Essex, CO3 0LP UK

Contents

All figures within this issue are available to view in colour free of charge online at http://dx.doi.org/10.1080/02681307.2022.2030975

Acknowledgements

The authors would like to thank RUSI's partners at the Securing Northern Europe Programme. This work is presented within the Security and Defence in Northern Europe research programme, funded by the Norwegian Ministry of Defence, and is a collaborative effort of the Norwegian Institute for Defence Studies, the Center for Strategic and International Studies, the German Council on Foreign Relations and RUSI.

About the Authors

Sidharth Kaushal is a Research Fellow, Sea Power at RUSI. He holds a doctorate in International Relations from the London School of Economics, where his research examined the ways in which strategic culture shapes the contours of a nation's grand strategy.

James Byrne is a Senior Research Fellow in the Proliferation and Nuclear Policy programme at RUSI.

Joe Byrne is a Research Analyst in the Proliferation and Nuclear Policy programme at RUSI.

Giangiuseppe Pili is a Research Fellow for RUSI's Project Sandstone.

Gary Somerville is a Research Analyst in the Proliferation and Nuclear Policy programme at RUSI.

INTRODUCTION

The impact of climate change, coupled with the resurgence of great power competition in Europe, will have a significant impact on the geopolitics of the Arctic and the High North – an area typically defined as including both the Arctic and the seas surrounding Scandinavia. The opening of the Northern Sea Route (NSR) with the melting of the Arctic ice cap creates both opportunities and risks for actors in what has been a low tension region since the end of the Cold War.[1] Cold War concerns, such as Russian and NATO fears that the other side's submarines could threaten vital interests and questions over how secure northern members of the Alliance are vis-à-vis Russia, have consequently resurfaced.[2]

The growing importance of the Arctic and High North is reflected in Russia's recent military build-up in the region, which has received an increasing share of expenditure from the Kremlin over the past decade. While a great deal has been done to examine the intentions behind this build-up, the authors of this paper have adopted a different approach. They have analysed the degree to which Russia's force structure, posture and infrastructure in the region can support alternative strategic and operational objectives. Beginning from a position of relative agnosticism about Moscow's objectives, the paper tests the ability of Russian capabilities to support a variety of plausible military and strategic aims in the region by examining the balance of power between Russian and NATO forces. The paper begins with the assumption that capabilities are a surer guide on which to base NATO policy than intentions.[3] The key findings of the paper are:

---

[1] Mathieu Boulègue, *Russia's Military Posture in the Arctic: Managing Hard Power in a 'Low Tension' Environment* (London: Chatham House, 2019).
[2] On the Cold War dynamics of the High North, see Barry R Posen, *Inadvertent Escalation: Conventional War and Nuclear Issues* (Ithaca, NY: Cornell University Press, 1991), pp. 155–61.
[3] On the theoretical reasoning behind this assumption, see John Mearsheimer, *The Tragedy of Great Power Politics* (New York, NY: W W Norton, 2001). Intentions certainly matter, but given their relative fluidity, are difficult to predict. By contrast, capabilities are relatively stable and can be used to predict the upper

- Over the next decade, Russia will enjoy effective peacetime control over most of the High North.
- In a conflict scenario, while not dominant, Russia enjoys significant offensive advantages over NATO, both within and immediately beyond the Arctic Circle.
- Russia is also challenged, however, by asymmetrical vulnerabilities in the region, which could be exploited by a NATO military approach that emphasises power projection in the region to target Russia's asymmetrical vulnerabilities.
- Both Russia and Western actors will have an incentive to take significant risks in the region, particularly when it comes to subsurface warfare. This poses challenges for maintaining strategic stability.

The authors have conducted an exhaustive survey of Russia's regional capabilities, which reveals several strengths and weaknesses. Russia's investment in base infrastructure, including a string of air and other bases on Alexandra Land and Kotelny Island, will allow it to maintain a near permanent presence on the NSR.

Moreover, Russia's capabilities in the western portions of its Arctic coastline include a dense integrated air-defence system, an increasingly capable submarine fleet and improvements to the capabilities and supporting infrastructure of assets such as the Backfire bomber. These capabilities will allow Moscow to escalate its dominance early on in a conflict with NATO, if it spreads to the high north coastline of Russia. Further east, by contrast, Russia's air-defence network is less dense, raising the prospect of vulnerability to Allied strategic bombers. Russia's Far East is much less heavily defended than its west, although it does benefit from the fact that the Bering Strait is a natural, and highly defendable, chokepoint. This being said, should NATO expand a conflict that began in Europe beyond the region, the Central Arctic and the Russian Far East could become a source of vulnerabilities.

Russia's control over its High North is thus far from certain. The country has significant vulnerabilities, including the lack of capable anti-submarine warfare (ASW) assets and a relatively thin air-defence shield over the Central Arctic, which could be used by NATO to target asymmetric Russian vulnerabilities. These include, but are not limited to, its critical infrastructure in the region. Russian fears of Western strike capabilities against its own Arctic territory are therefore well founded. Should NATO opt to embrace horizontal escalation in the event of a

---

bounds of an actor's ambition. States naturally gravitate towards this in an uncertain international environment in which it is difficult to ascertain intentions.

conflict with Russia, it may well find the Arctic and High North a region in which it enjoys significant opportunities.

The purpose of this paper is to generate a systematic first cut examination of the balance of power in the Arctic and High North. The paper seeks to outline the maximal level of ambition that Russia's current force structure can sustain, rather than examining the scope of Russian ambition, which is the subject of another lengthy debate. This will provide an evidence base for subsequent analysis, wargaming and policy discussions.

Methodology

This paper relies on using a mix of methods. The authors have conducted an extensive open-source intelligence effort. These methods include the use of satellite imagery triangulated with sources such as Russian-language news and a review of secondary sources to arrive at deductions regarding Moscow's capabilities in the region. Existing sources of information of the Russian military, including the International Institute for Strategic Studies' *The Military Balance 2020*, provide a useful first cut by articulating aggregate platform numbers. However, there is room to expand on the data available by examining factors such as the geographical disposition of assets and readiness.

The authors began by surveying the secondary literature on Russia's force dispositions conducted by organisations such as the Center for Strategic and International Studies and the Georgian Foundation for Strategic and International Studies (also known as the Rondeli Foundation). In addition, published articles from both Russian- and English-language news outlets about the movement of platforms within the region were surveyed. This served an orienting function, narrowing search parameters to the likely locations of specific capabilities. This, in turn, enabled the authors to use satellite imagery derived with support from Maxar technologies to verify readiness and dispositions, as well as the introduction of new platforms to the region. For example, vessels' readiness was established by examining imagery of them at bases, as opposed to in shipyards such as Sevmash. Searches for platforms such as anti-access capabilities and air-defence systems were conducted first by examining large swathes of data with a high level of detail and subsequently investigating areas of interest with higher-quality imagery. Cross-referencing the imagery analysis conducted by the authors with existing literature and the locations of known Russian formations in the region allowed for a more detailed picture of capabilities in the region. This both synthesised existing sources and added to the information provided through imagery of new and emerging capabilities in the region to be created.

The authors were able to therefore compile a comprehensive database of Russia's force structure, capabilities and infrastructure generated in the region over the past decade. The database includes the locations of all the units in the region and their likely capabilities. While it is impractical to include the entirety of the authors' database or all their imagery in this paper, key samples are included throughout and all of the data is presented in a series of infographics. The authors have also relied on a literature review of secondary sources, including assessments of NATO readiness prepared by various organisations.

Finally, the authors have conducted campaign analysis to arrive at deductions about the balance of power in each military domain considered. For the purposes of this paper, these are the air, subsurface, surface and ground domains. Campaign analysis is a multidisciplinary tool, which incorporates formal modelling, scenario analysis and qualitative research. Its unifying thread – which distinguishes it from long-term forecasting tools, such as net assessment – is the importance placed on specifying time, geographical and capability parameters.[4] The specific analytical tools used by the authors vary by chapter. The authors sought, where possible, to use formal models to get answers about the relative balance of forces. However, both deterministic and stochastic models have their limitations, which become particularly acute in specific domains such as ground warfare, where the number of interacting variables including but not limited to the number of individual components (troops or tanks, for example) and the impact of complex terrain tend to confound efforts at modelling.[5] As such, the paper uses a wide-ranging methodological approach to assessing the military balance in each domain, combining both formal modelling and tabletop operations analysis.

It is worth noting that while campaign analysis can only inform the authors' assessments of higher-intensity scenarios, the relative balance of power between the two actors concerning these scenarios will likely shape dynamics elsewhere. Competition, in effect, is conducted under the backdrop of high-intensity conflict and the degree of confidence in one's ability to prevail in the latter shapes the former.[6]

---

[4] For a useful discussion of campaign analysis, see Rachel Tescott and Andrew Halterman, 'The Case for Campaign Analysis: A Method for Studying Military Operations', *International Security* (Vol. 45, No. 4, Spring 2021), pp. 44–83.

[5] Andrew Illachinski, 'Land Warfare and Complexity, Part II: An Assessment of the Applicability of Nonlinear Dynamics and Complex Systems Theory to the Study of Land Warfare (U)', Center for Naval Analyses, 1996.

[6] On this symbiotic relationship, particularly in Russian thinking, see Stephen R Covington, 'The Culture of Strategic Thought Behind Russia's Modern Approaches to Warfare', Belfer Center for Science and International Affairs, Harvard Kennedy School, Defense and Intelligence Projects, 2016, pp. 1–10.

Structure

The paper examines the balance of military capabilities and related scenario specific dynamics in four distinct military domains: ocean surface; subsurface; air; and land. The chapters are modular by design and can be read independently. While each domain is considered individually, the interrelationships between them in areas such as joint sensors and fires are discussed throughout. While not providing a formal coded score denoting relative military advantage, as similar previous works have done, each chapter contains a discussion of the balance of power in a particular area.[7] The paper concludes with a discussion of the implications of the individual power balances assessed in each chapter.

---

[7] For example, Eric Heginbotham et al., *The U.S.–China Military Scorecard: Forces, Geography, and the Evolving Balance of Power 1996–2017* (Santa Monica, CA: RAND, 2015).

CHAPTER I: THE STRATEGIC CONTEXT

Key Points

- The impact of climate change over the next decade will create both opportunities and challenges for Arctic states.
- Russia, in particular, will face a combination of economic challenges and military vulnerabilities.
- In addition to traditional concerns regarding the preservation of Russia's strategic deterrent, the protection of its infrastructure in an increasingly economically significant region will be critical for the country.
- Effective control over the NSR could potentially turn this into a significant revenue generator for the Russian state.
- Should a high-intensity conflict either erupt in the High North or spread there as a result of conflict between Russia and NATO elsewhere, a combination of offensive and defensive considerations, including mutual weaknesses in the area of ASW between Russia and NATO, incentivise – but do not necessarily predetermine – a competitive security dilemma in a previously low-tension region.

The coming decade will see significant changes in the Arctic region, as the effects of climate change alter the economic and strategic geography of the region. The opening of the NSR and increased access to mineral deposits within the region is a significant economic opportunity for states in the Arctic Circle. Simultaneously, however, this has the potential to intensify geopolitical competition in what has traditionally been a low-tension region. Disagreements over freedom of navigation could lead to conflict. Consider, for example, recent legislation in Russia stipulating that vessels sailing the NSR must secure permission from Moscow and use the services of Russian icebreakers and pilots. Foreign Minister Sergei Lavrov and former Deputy Prime Minister Dimitri Rogozin noted that control over a potentially vital maritime artery could represent a strategic opportunity for Russia, as well as an economic one.[1] The

---

[1] Nastassia Astrasheuskaya and Henry Foy, 'Polar Powers: Russia's Bid for Supremacy in the Arctic Ocean', *Financial Times*, 27 April 2019; Michael Peck, 'Russia Has a Plan to Dominate the Arctic', *National Interest*, 7 January 2018.

potential threat to freedom of navigation that this might pose was noted by figures such as former US Secretary of State Mike Pompeo, Curtis Scaparrotti, the former SACEUR, and former US Secretary of the Navy Richard Spencer.[2] The recently released US Navy Arctic Strategy also reflects an apprehension that the region may become a domain of maritime competition in the future.[3]

Another factor worthy of consideration is the impact of a more navigable Arctic on the security of countries, including Russia, which has substantial regional economic interests and moreover has historically relied on the relative inaccessibility of the region in order to shield the undersea component of its nuclear triad.[4] The threat to its undersea deterrent, as well as a perception that there exists a northern gap in Russian air and missile defences doubtless gives understandable incentives to military investments by Moscow.

Finally, conflict could spread to the region as a result of developments elsewhere. A clash between Russia and NATO in the Baltics or the Black Sea could become multiregional. This could impact the High North in a number of ways. Russia would likely attempt to sortie some of its submarines from the region to threaten NATO shipping in the wider Atlantic and, perhaps, other critical infrastructure. Alternatively, NATO might decide to offset Russian strengths in other regions, such as the Baltics, through horizontal escalation on its maritime periphery, much as the Reagan-era maritime strategy envisioned.

Recent years have seen Russia invest substantially in military infrastructure within the Arctic. Russia has reactivated or built 13 air bases within the region. Moscow has placed capabilities such as the S-400 SAM and the Bastion-P anti-ship missile systems in the area. In addition, the Northern Fleet based at Murmansk has been elevated to the status of a Joint Strategic Command, with control over a range of ground, air- and sea-based assets, as well as responsibility for Russia's Arctic Islands such as Alexandra Land and Kotelny. These trends all point to the growing prominence of the Arctic within Russia's strategic outlook.

Analysts have expressed different opinions about the motivations for this build-up. Some suggest a desire to dominate the region and use it as a springboard for power projection into the Atlantic. Others have noted that essentially defensive motivations may well be driving Russian activity and

---

[2] Malte Humpert, 'US Navy Plans to Send Naval Vessels Through the Arctic', *ArcticToday*, 12 March 2019.
[3] For a copy of the strategy, see *USNI News*, 'New Navy, Marine Corps Strategic Blueprint for the Arctic', 5 January 2021.
[4] Boulègue, *Russia's Military Posture in the Arctic*.

that its regional posture may be a reactive one.[5] In many ways, the ambiguity regarding intentions mirrors the discourse of the past two decades over other regions such as the South China Sea. There, the motivations ascribed to the People's Republic of China range from the creation of a safe bastion for vulnerable ballistic missile submarines (SSBNs) to offset Beijing's vulnerability in this area through to more expansive attempts at regional hegemony.[6]

The fact that capabilities can serve both defensive and revisionist objectives has the effect of limiting the degree to which insights about national intent can be gleaned from capability investments. Capabilities that can serve defensive aims - such as air-defence systems or coastal missile batteries, to name two – can also create zones of denial for another state's assets and thus enable regional revisionism.

The paper therefore aims to answer a different question: what is the maximum level of ambition that Russia's emergent Arctic force structure can sustain? The purpose of this paper is to use the tools of campaign analysis to provide a coarse look at the balance of power between Russia and NATO in a series of three potential scenarios, rather than attempting to infer Moscow's ambitions:

1 Peacetime competition between NATO and Russia over disputes on freedom of navigation in the Arctic. This would be similar to the below-the-threshold-of-warfare situation between Russia and NATO in the Black Sea or Sino–American competition in the South China Sea.
2 A Russian attempt to project power from the Arctic into adjoining areas such as the Barents and Norwegian Seas, as well as the Atlantic, in the context of a conflict with NATO. The purpose of this scenario is to assess Russia's offensive capabilities in the region.
3 A NATO attempt to project power into Russian-controlled parts of the Arctic in wartime, comparable to that envisioned under the Reagan administration's Maritime Strategy.[7]

---

[5] For examples of each view, see Matthew Melino and Heather Conley, 'The Ice Curtain: Russia's Arctic Military Presence', Center for Strategic and International Studies; Boulègue, *Russia's Military Posture in the Arctic*.
[6] For examples of each view, see Bernard Cole, *The Great Wall at Sea: China's Navy Enters the Twenty-First Century* (Annapolis, MD: Naval Institute Press, 2010), p. 125; James Holmes and Toshi Yoshihara, *Red Star Over the Pacific: China's Rise and the Challenge to U.S. Maritime Strategy* (Annapolis, MD: Naval Institute Press, 2018).
[7] The Reagan administration's Maritime Strategy envisioned using NATO's preponderance at sea to offset the USSR's advantages on land in the event of a conflict. Had war broken out, the concept envisioned, among other things, NATO surface and subsurface assets threatening Soviet capabilities in and around the Kola Peninsula – thereby compelling the USSR to de-escalate before its ground

The authors base these scenarios on two parameters: broad plausibility; and the degree to which they can serve as proxies for the balance of power in the region. If, for example, Russia can be seen as prevailing in both the offensive and defensive conflict scenarios, it would imply a high level of control over the region. It is worth noting that two factors could have an effect on the results of the authors' analysis: the ability of either side to conduct a preparatory build-up; and the degree to which either NATO or Russian forces can be redeployed from other regions. To control for the first, the authors consider both scenarios in which Russia initiates hostilities and scenarios in which NATO conducts a build-up in line with the three 30s commitments of NATO's readiness initiative.[8] The second is more difficult to control, insofar as it depends in part on the commitments of NATO and Russia in other regions. In each scenario, therefore, the authors vary available force numbers to reflect different possible levels of extra regional force allocation, using exercises, such as *Trident Juncture, Dynamic Mongoose* and *Steadfast Protector,* to inform the analysis.

The first scenario, in which Russian and Western assets engage in peacetime competition, is consistent with the ambitions suggested by official statements and Moscow's recent navigation laws.[9] It would entail a degree of competition and assertiveness by Russia over what it regards as its sovereign rights in the region, according to its interpretation of the United Nations Convention on the Law of the Sea (UNCLOS), but not necessarily offensive intent insofar as these rights do have some basis in international and domestic law.

The second scenario, in which Russia attempts to both deny NATO access to the Arctic in a conflict and to use it as a springboard for operations in the Atlantic, could materialise in the context of a Russia–NATO clash that began beyond the region. For example, if a clash erupted in the Baltics, it could quickly spread beyond the region. This is similar to the Cold War scenario, when it was assumed that a clash in

---

forces could achieve a breakthrough. See John Hattendorf et al., *The Evolution of the U.S. Navy's Maritime Strategy 1977–1986* (Newport, RI: US Naval War College, 2004).

[8] The NATO readiness initiative commits the Alliance to generate 30 vessels, 30 squadrons of aircraft and 30 mechanised battalions within 30 days of conflict. See NATO, 'Press Conference by NATO Secretary General Jens Stoltenberg Following the Meeting of NATO Defence Ministers', 24 October 2019, <https://www.nato.int/cps/en/natohq/opinions_169936.htm>, accessed 28 November 2021.

[9] Atle Staalsen, 'Russia Sets Out Stringent New Rules for Foreign Ships on the Northern Sea Route', *Arctic Today,* 8 March 2019, <https://www.arctictoday.com/russia-sets-out-stringent-new-rules-for-foreign-ships-on-the-northern-sea-route/>, accessed 28 November 2021.

central Germany would quickly spread to the High North as the Soviet Union attempted to neutralise Norwegian airfields and use its submarines to challenge Atlantic sea lines of communication (SLOCs). Today, the submarines of Russia's Northern Fleet and Directorate of Deep Sea Research (GUGI), as well as strategic bombers based in the Arctic, could play a similar role. Doing so would be consistent with a Russian approach geared towards regional dominance within the Arctic and contestation of the areas adjoining it.

The third scenario is consistent with a Russian posture that is defensive with respect to the Arctic – but not necessarily with other regions – and a Western approach geared towards imposing greater levels of competitive pressure on Russia in the region to offset vulnerabilities elsewhere. This broadly mirrors the late Cold War during which the Reagan administration attempted to pressure Russia in the High North by using Western maritime strengths to offset perceived land-based Soviet advantages in central Europe.

The participation of non-NATO members such as Finland might be worthy of discussion too, or that bilateral interactions matter more in the High North. While this is true, the authors assume that NATO must be the framework for Western engagement in the region, given the lack of capacity in the area. The balance of power between Russia and NATO will therefore be key to determining the dynamics of bilateral interactions, in which Western actors' positions will be determined by this equation. For the purposes of this paper, these beliefs will serve as a baseline assumption.

It is worth noting that the authors attempt to maintain a degree of neutrality as to actors' intentions and future strategies. The paper's purpose is to provide an overview of key aspects of the strategic balance in the region, against which future developments can be measured. Although the Western Arctic in and around the Kola Peninsula has received priority in terms of scenario-based assessments of this balance of power, the paper discusses developments in the other parts of the Russian Arctic as well as their strategic significance.

Russian Interests in the Arctic

The Arctic has substantial economic and strategic importance for Russia. The Russian Arctic accounts for 20% of the country's exports, and contains 10% of its fossil-fuel deposits.[10] It also accounts for all of Russia's diamonds, stibium, apatite, phlogopite, vermiculite, rare and rare earth metals, as well as platinum, nickel, cobalt and

---

[10] Eugene Rumer, Richard Sokolsky and Paul Stronski, 'Russia in the Arctic – A Critical Examination', Carnegie Endowment for International Peace, March 2021.

copper.[11] Russia's Arctic strategy envisions the attraction of capital to the region to unlock this economic potential as climate change makes assets such as hydrocarbon deposits increasingly accessible.[12]

The Arctic has substantial economic and strategic importance for Russia. The Russian Arctic contains an estimated 86 trillion cubic metres of gas and 13 billion tons of oil resources.[13] These deposits are crucial for Russia's export-oriented energy industry, which the country's most recent official planning document described as the 'central pillar of Russia's economy in the upcoming decade'.[14]

Facing a growing drive in Europe to move away from fossil fuels, the long-term future of Russian gas on the continent – its largest historical client – looks bleak.[15] As a result, Russia has already begun diversifying its export base, building liquefied natural gas (LNG) facilities on the Yamal Peninsula, in the Arctic. This multibillion-dollar facility uses special ice-class carriers to run the eastern part of the NSR, delivering gas to clients in Asia, the world's largest growing market. Russia plans to expand this facility and build a number of other LNG plants in the Arctic, further developing its resource base for exports to Asian markets.[16]

The area also accounts for the production of 100% of Russia's diamonds, stibium, apatite, phlogopite, vermiculite, rare and rare earth metals, as well as platinum, nickel cobalt copper.[17]

Given that a great deal of Russian military literature underscores the importance of protecting critical infrastructure against the risk posed by, among other things, adversary air and naval power, the defence of this

---

[11] Valery Pilyavsky, 'The Arctic: Russia's Economic and Geopolitical Interests', Briefing Paper, Friedrich Ebert Stiftung, March 2011.

[12] Janis Kluge and Michael Paul, *Russia's Arctic Strategy Through to 2035: Grand Ambitions and Pragmatic Constraints* (Berlin: Stiftung Wissenschaft und Politik, 2020); Emily Ferris, 'Problems of Geography: Military and Economic Transport Logistics in Russia's Far East', *RUSI Occasional Papers* (October 2020).

[13] Elias G Carayannis, Alina Ilinova and Alexey Cherepovitsyn, 'The Future of Energy and the Case of the Arctic Offshore: The Role of Strategic Management', *Journal of Marine Science and Engineering* (Vol. 9, No. 2, 2021).

[14] Sergey Sukhankin, 'Russia's Energy Strategy 2035: A Breakthrough or Another Impasse?' *Eurasia Daily Monitor* (Vol. 17, No. 78, 2020).

[15] Vitaly Yermakov, 'Russian Gas: The Year of Living Dangerously: Key Takeaways for 2020 and Beyond', Oxford Institute for Energy Studies, September 2020, <https://www.oxfordenergy.org/wpcms/wp-content/uploads/2020/09/Russian-Gas-the-year-of-living-dangerously.pdf>, accessed 7 November.

[16] James Henderson and Vitaly Yermakov, 'Russian LNG: Becoming a Global Force', Oxford Institute for Energy Studies, November 2019, <https://www.oxfordenergy.org/wpcms/wp-content/uploads/2019/11/Russian-LNG-Becoming-a-Global-Force-NG-154.pdf>, accessed 7 November 2021.

[17] Michael Kofman, speech given at RUSI Seapower Conference, London, 25 February 2021.

economic heartland is likely to be central to Moscow's military planning.[18] Russian policy in the region is geared towards the need for an early and persistent presence in the region, to assert Moscow's claims to administrative control of the NSR.[19]

The opening of the NSR, which could slash transit times between Asia and Europe by up to 30%, represents another economic opportunity for Russia – particularly if it can act in a rent-seeking role by making its services invaluable (and irreplaceable) to vessels transiting this route. This was the likely rationale behind laws such as Russia's 2013 legislation which stipulates that vessels transiting the NSR must use the services of Russian icebreakers and pilots and a 2017 law prohibiting the movement of hydrocarbons using the route on non-Russian vessels.[20] The Arctic also contains significant Russian military interests. Eight of Russia's SSBNs (six *Delta*-class and two *Borei*-class) are allotted to the Northern Fleet, and the defence of these assets is a key objective for the military.[21] While it is unlikely, at the time of writing, that any state would wish to target this leg of Russia's nuclear triad, it is worth noting that during the 1980s US maritime strategy envisioned doing precisely this.[22] Russian fears that this threat may materialise in the future are therefore not entirely unreasonable.

The Arctic is also a springboard for offensive activity. The Northern Fleet Joint Strategic Command (OSK Sever) holds 20% of Russia's precision strike capability in peacetime, and possesses the launch platforms of all its air-launched Kinzhal ballistic missiles.[23] It is likely that it would play a significant role in any conventional precision strike campaign that erupted following an escalation either in the Arctic or beyond. Its nuclear attack submarines, as well as the special-purpose submarines of GUGI, can play a range of roles, from stopping flows of

---

[18] *Ibid.*

[19] Sergey Sukhankin, 'The Military Pillar of Russia's Arctic Policy', *Eurasia Daily Monitor* (Vol. 17, No. 33, 2020).

[20] Pavel Devyatkin, 'Russia's Arctic Strategy: Maritime Shipping (Part IV)', Arctic Institute, 27 February 2018, <https://www.thearcticinstitute.org/russias-arctic-strategy-maritime-shipping-part-iv/>, accessed 1 April 2021.

[21] Ernie Regehr, 'Military Infrastructure and Strategic Capabilities: Russia's Arctic Defense Posture', in Daniel Hamilton, Kristina Spohr and Jason Moyer (eds), *The Arctic and World Order* (Washington, DC: Brookings Institution Press, 2021), p. 196.

[22] John Mearsheimer, 'A Strategic Misstep: The Maritime Strategy and Deterrence in Europe', *International Security* (Vol. 11, No. 2, Fall 1986), pp. 3–57.

[23] Tomas Malmof and Johan Engvall, 'Russia's Military Capability in a Ten-Year Perspective' in Frederik Westerlund and Susanna Oxenstierna (eds), *Russian Military Capability in a Ten Year Perspective – 2019* (Stockholm: FOI, 2019), p. 191. Note that whether these missiles are mated to platforms like the Tu-22M3 is unknown at the time of writing.

Figure 1: Russia's Critical Economic Infrastructure in the Arctic

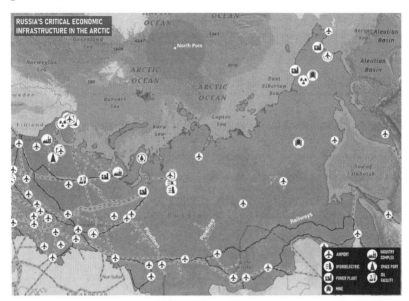

Source: Author generated

Figure 2: *Delta-, Akula-* and *Borei*-Class Submarines Present at Gadzhiyevo Naval Base on 1 May 2021

Source: Airbus Defence and Space and authors'

supplies into Europe to tapping or cutting key undersea cables or conducting long-range cruise missile attacks from unexpected vectors in forward positions.[24] During the Cold War, it was widely assumed that in the event of a conflict in central Europe, the Soviet Union would seek to conduct ground attacks to neutralise major air bases in Norway that threatened Murmansk.[25]

Rather than attempting to conclusively work out Moscow's intentions, this paper considers the ability of Russia's current Arctic force structure to support three distinct sets of objectives, which conform to three different levels of geopolitical ambition. The first, minimal objective set concerns the defence of Russia's critical military and civilian assets against an external attack. The second considers Russian efforts to place parts of the High North and NSR under Russian law, in addition to the military defensive objectives. Finally, the authors consider the ability of Russia's current force structure to support both control over the Arctic and power projection into the wider High North and the Atlantic during a short conflict in Europe.

The current balance of power will evolve as both Russian and NATO capabilities develop. The purpose of this paper is to provide an insight into the baseline balance of power for both parties both in peacetime and following a period of mobilisation. This is to provide a snapshot of the balance of power against which future developments can be measured. The authors discuss the evolution of the balance of power on a domain specific basis. However, each chapter includes discussions about the interrelationships between specific domains.

---

[24] The GUGI is a unique organisation that emphasises undersea intelligence gathering, as well as certain special operations such as disrupting sensor networks. See Globalsecurity, 'Main Directorate of Deep Sea Research (Military Unit 40056)', <https://www.globalsecurity.org/intell/world/russia/gugi.htm>, accessed 29 November 2021.
[25] Posen, *Inadvertent Escalation*, pp. 155–61.

CHAPTER II: THE BALANCE OF CAPABILITIES IN THE SUBSURFACE DOMAIN

Key Points

- Despite a quantitative decline since the collapse of the Soviet Union, there have been several qualitative improvements in Russia's submarine force that partially offset this fact.
- The force now has a number of missions which may not require it to sortie far from the Arctic. These include conducting precision strikes against ground targets at long ranges and, potentially, exerting sea control over the NSR. Simply placing forces in the Greenland-Iceland-UK (GIUK) Gap is not an adequate riposte to this force.
- In the models run to inform the campaign analysis in this chapter, both Russian and NATO submarines are effective at penetrating each other's ASW barriers. For NATO, this incentivises a forward posture in a conflict with Russia. On the one hand, a reactive posture emphasising containing Russian submarines may lead to failure while an offensive posture can exploit Russia's asymmetrical vulnerabilities.
- The subsurface environment has a rough, but highly offence-dominated balance of power.

Russia's Northern Fleet submarines have been a mainstay of its maritime force posture during the Soviet era and since. The defence of the maritime component of Russia's nuclear triad has historically been the primary focus of this force, with the interdiction of Atlantic SLOCs in wartime occupying a secondary role.[1] Post-Cold War, however, the changing maritime geography of the Arctic, as well as the evolution of

---

[1] Hattendorf, *The Evolution of the U.S. Navy's Maritime Strategy, 1977–86*, pp. 23–30.

Russia's strategic position, have incentivised an evolution of the Northern Fleet's subsurface capabilities and missions.

After a post-Cold War trough in its capabilities, which saw the Russian navy's submarine force shrink in size from 266 operational boats in 1991 to 64 in 2000, the fleet embarked on a process of modernisation to restore both capacity and capability.[2] While the number of vessels in service is smaller, modernisation under the Russian Federation's 10-year state armament plan, launched in 2010, have increased the lethality of the force. The Russian navy was the largest beneficiary of the 2010 State Armament Plan, receiving 26.3% of the roughly RUB10 trillion (about $140 billion) allocated between 2011 and 2020.[3] This expenditure has underpinned the progress of ambitious projects, such as the *Yasen*-class and *Yasen-M*-class guided missile submarines (SSGNs), Russia's most advanced nuclear-powered submarines to date. The Russian navy is also no longer alone in the subsurface space. It has been joined by GUGI, which fields a number of special purpose submarines, including the *Belogorod* and *Khabarovsk* – two modified *Oscar*-class SSGNs that can act as motherships for deep-sea surveillance assets. These include the Harpsichord UUV (unmanned underwater vehicle) and the *Losharik* – a specialised deep-diving vessel — which can carry the nuclear-armed Poseidon torpedo.[4] These assets enable the Russian submarine force to act in a variety of clandestine activities, from placing underwater sensors to the disruption of an adversary's sensor networks and undersea cables.

While the decline in the number of submarines in the Russian navy has continued, this has been offset by qualitative improvements in the force. As of 2016, the Northern Fleet was estimated to comprise 24 active submarines, excluding SSBNs.[5] The Pacific fleet, which controls the other major route of egress from the Arctic, has six SSGNs and four *Akula*-class attack submarines (SSNs), as well as 11 *Kilo*-class diesel-electrics (SSKs), two of which are the modern improved Kilo.

The mission set of the Russian navy's submarines has evolved in a number of ways. While the protection of SSBNs remains paramount, the Russian submarine fleet has taken on a number of additional roles. The force has followed the rest of the navy by embracing a role in a

---

[2] Arnaud Sobrero, 'Russian Submarines, Still a Relevant Threat?', *The Diplomat*, 11 February 2021.
[3] Julian Cooper, *Russia's State Armament Programme to 2020: A Quantitative Assessment of Implementation 2011–2015* (Stockholm: FOI, 2016), p. 20.
[4] Globalsecurity, 'Main Directorate of Deep-Sea Research: (Military Unit 40056)', <https://www.globalsecurity.org/intell/world/russia/gugi.htm>, accessed 7 November 2021.
[5] Andrew Metrick, Kathleen Weinberger and Kathleen Hicks, *Undersea Warfare in Northern Europe* (Washington, DC: CSIS, 2016), pp. 11–12.

Figure 3: Submarine Bases of the Northern Fleet

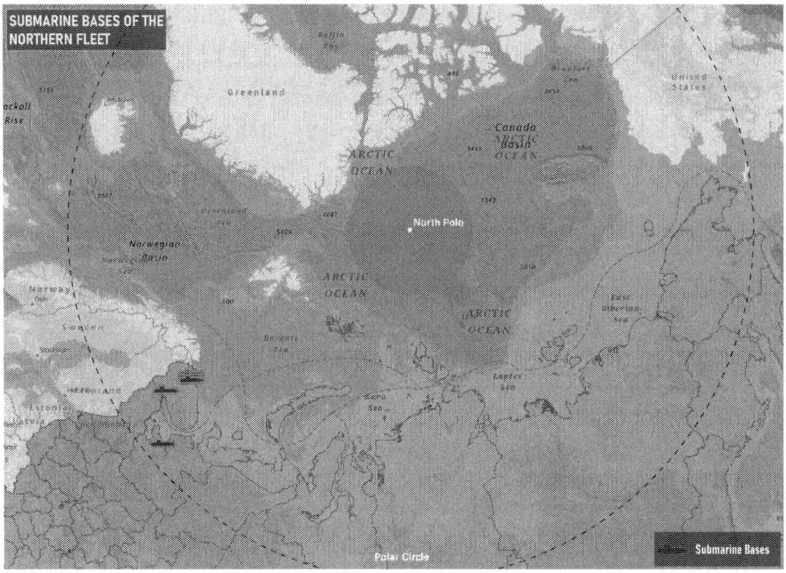

Source: Author generated

conventional precision strike campaign. Its newest *Yasen*-class nuclear submarines have a Vertical Launch System (VLS) capacity that hold up to 40 Kalibr land-attack missiles.[6] Precision strike is crucial to Russia's approach to localising conventional wars on its periphery – both by inflicting calibrated 'assigned damage' on an adversary's society and by slowing the pace of deployment.[7] The ability to launch conventionally armed precision strike assets is therefore highly beneficial to a service seeking to stake its claim to limited national resources. The Russian navy has effectively made a case for itself as a force capable of conducting a full spectrum of strike operations ranging from conventional precision strikes to low-yield nuclear strikes and, at the top of the escalation ladder, strategic nuclear strikes. Its subsurface assets are central to its ability to play this role.[8] Russian military science scholarship reveals a fear of foreign powers conducting a conventional strike campaign against the country's interior.[9]

In addition to this function, subsurface assets will be critical to any Russian effort to exert control over the NSR. While it is true that

---

[6]   Eric Werheim, 'Russia's Capable New SSGN', US Naval Institute, May 2020.
[7]   Michael Kofman and Anya Fink, *Russian Strategy for Escalation Management: Key Concepts, Debates, and Players in Military Thought* (Arlington, VA: CAN, 2020).
[8]   Kofman, speech given at RUSI Seapower Conference.
[9]   *Ibid.*

submarines are less useful as a tool of presence missions than more visible surface vessels, a tacit understanding of the balance of power underneath the ocean's surface tends to shape the behaviour of competing parties.[10] For example, during the so-called 'Third Battle of the Atlantic', in which the US and USSR competed to secure an undersea advantage during the Cold War, both nations sought to demonstrate their ability to, respectively, break out into the ocean and deny their opponent the ability to do so. In other words, the subsurface balance of power is an 'elephant in the room', which shapes the behaviour of parties across a range of scenarios.[11]

Finally, it is likely that at least a portion of the Russian submarine fleet in the Arctic will attempt to break out of its bastions into the North Atlantic in crisis and wartime, though analysts debate the relative weight placed on this mission.[12] Special purpose submarines such as the GUGI-controlled *Belgorod* can potentially play a crucial role in a range of scenarios given potential coercive value of their ability to impact the functioning of undersea cables. Similarly, if Russian Arctic-based SSGNs manage to get into the Norwegian Sea or the Atlantic, they could in principle threaten infrastructure such as bases hosting NATO's tanker fleet in wartime.

The presumed missions in which Russia's submarines are therefore expected to be involved are, in order of importance:

- SSBN protection.
- Controlling the routes of ingress to the NSR.
- Disruptive operations beyond the Arctic.

The Capabilities of Russia and NATO

Russia

The Russian submarine force in the Arctic is based on the assets of the Pacific and Northern Fleets. From their headquarters at Vladivostok and Severomorsk, these fleets control 42 submarines (excluding SSBNs). Numbers on paper are not always reflective of real capabilities. For example, only three of the five *Oscar*-class SSGNs held by the Pacific Fleet are operational, while four of its five *Akula*-class SSNs are either

---

[10] James P Stebbins, *Broaching the Ship: Rethinking Submarines as a Signalling Tool in Naval Diplomacy* (Monterey, CA: Naval Postgraduate School, 2015).

[11] Owen R Cote Jr, *The Third Battle: Innovation in the U.S. Navy's Silent Cold War Struggle With Soviet Submarines* (Newport, RI: US Naval War College, 2003).

[12] For a discussion of Russian objectives, see Metrick, Weinberger and Hicks, *Undersea Warfare in Northern Europe*; Kofman, speech at RUSI Seapower Conference. Analysts tend to agree that both bastion defence and SLOC interdiction will play a role in Russian maritime strategy, with differences of opinion over the relative weight given each function.

inactive or awaiting repair.[13] According to previous analysis on this subject, seven of the Northern Fleet's 14 SSNs were active.[14] Nonetheless, the two relevant Arctic fleets possess a powerful subsurface force. This is particularly true considering that the capabilities of Moscow's opponents have deteriorated faster than Russia's own subsurface forces, as will be demonstrated in this chapter.[15] While fewer in number than at any time in its post-1945 history, the Russian navy's submarines are becoming more versatile and capable. For example, the refitting of a number of vessels with the 3M-54 Kalibr will allow them to contribute to a precision strike campaign from the safety of Arctic bastions.[16] The opening of the NSR has made it possible for Russian planners to contemplate the easier movement of resources between the two previously disjointed fleets, perhaps leading to the creation of an integrated force.[17]

Older submarines such as the *Victor III* and *Sierra I* and *II* are relatively noisy, making them vulnerable to detection. The *Victor* was considered ahead of its time, equipped with capabilities such as a passive towed array sonar, but currently it is seen as having a sound profile comparable to relatively noisy SSNs such as the Chinese Type 093.[18] The titanium-hulled *Sierra II* is a quieter submarine, which may well have a noise profile comparable to the first generation of *Akula* submarines. The *Akula* was produced as a copy of the *Sierra* with the exception of a steel hull that made it easier to build. The *Sierra* carries the MGK-501 Skat passive-array sonar that is also found on *Akulas*, though newer versions carry the MGK-600.

The newer components of Russia's nuclear submarine force, comprised of *Akulas*, *Akula IIs* and *Yasens*, will likely pose a formidable challenge to ASW operators. The noise profile of the *Akula* is comparable to that of the US Navy's Los Angeles-class, while the *Improved Akula* and *Yasen* classes are, respectively, comparable to the

---

[13] Xavier Vavasseur. 'Russia's Pacific Fleet to Get 15 New Vessels in 2020', *Naval News*, 29 May 2020.
[14] Metrick, Weinberger and Hicks, *Undersea Warfare in Northern Europe*, p. 10; numbers validated by authors via imagery of key port and shipyards to identify vessels currently in refit.
[15] Julianne Smith and Jerry Hendrix, 'Forgotten Waters – Minding the GIUK Gap: A Tabletop Exercise', Center for a New American Security (CNAS), May 2017.
[16] See, for example, H I Sutton, 'Russian Submarine May Test New Missile off Norway This Week', *Forbes*, 26 October 2019; Xavier Vavasseur, 'Russia's Akula-Class Submarines to Fire Kalibr Cruise Missile Following Upgrade', *NavalNews*, 30 March 2020.
[17] Atle Staalesen, 'A Large-Scale Russian Military Exercise Is Coming to the Arctic', *Barents Observer*, 20 December 2018.
[18] The justifications for noise estimates are provided in the footnotes to Table 2.

Figure 4: *Oscar II-* Class SSGNs at the Zapadnaya Litsa Naval Base on 22 March 2021

Source: Airbus Defence and Space and authors'

Improved Los Angeles-class and *Seawolf*-class SSNs.[19] In addition to carrying heavy torpedoes, these submarines are increasingly being adapted to launch long-range strike assets. The *Yasen*, for example, will be able to launch the supersonic P-800 anti-ship cruise missile from its vertical launch cells, and can also launch the 3M22 Zircon. The P-800 will also replace the older P-700 Granit on the Northern Fleet's *Oscar*-Class submarines.[20] These submarines could threaten surface vessels up to 400 km away – beyond their ASW pickets – with assets that will give air defenders limited warning times.

In addition to nuclear submarines, Russia has a large number of diesel-electrics, including the Project 877 (Kilo) and Project 639.3 (Improved Kilo). It is also in the process of developing its next generation *Lada*-class SSK.[21] Diesel-electric submarines cannot

---

[19] See Eugene Miasnikov, 'The Future of Russia's Strategic Nuclear Forces: Discussions and Arguments', Federation for American Scientists, January 1997, <https://fas.org/spp/eprint/snf0322.htm>, accessed 12 March 2021.
[20] H I Sutton, 'Pr885 Severodvinsk Class', *Covert Shores*, 13 April 2019.
[21] NTI, 'Russia's Submarine Capabilities', fact sheet, 9 June 2014, <https://www.nti.org/analysis/articles/russia-submarine-capabilities/>, accessed 8 November 2021.

Figure 5: *Victor III*-Class and *Sierra II*-Class Submarines at Vidyayevo Naval Base, 11 February 2021

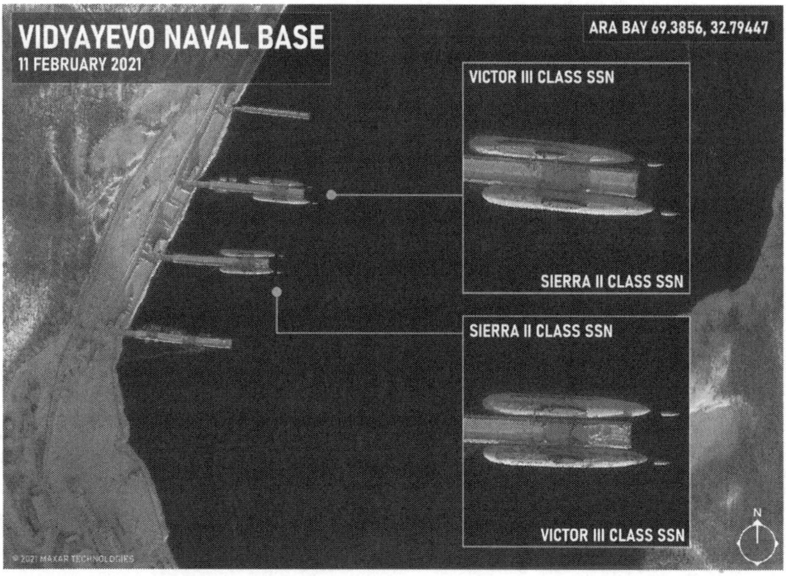

Source: Maxar Technologies and authors'

undertake long voyages but can provide a regional presence and potentially free nuclear-powered vessels for missions further afield. While Russian SSKs have lagged behind Western counterparts in areas such as air independent propulsion, newer models, such as the *Improved Kilo*, possess a sophisticated suite of quieting technologies and can pose a real threat to surface vessels as well as certain submarines.[22] *Kilos* can also carry up to four 3M-54 Kalibr missiles. They can therefore pose a risk to surface assets from ranges that exceed their traditional ASW pickets and can also participate in land-attack campaigns.[23] All Project 636 submarines will be Kalibr capable. The older project 877 SSKs, on the other hand, do not necessarily have this capacity, though some of the Northern Fleet's Project 877s are likely to have received it following refits.[24] [25]

---

[22] Franz-Stefan Gady, 'Confirmed: The Russian Pacific Fleet to Receive 6 New Attack Submarines', *The Diplomat*, 9 September 2016.
[23] Peter Suciu, 'Russian Submarine Fired Kalibr Missiles During Recent Exercise', *National Interest*, 29 September 2020.
[24] *PortNews*, 'SSK Kaluga to be Launched on May 26 After Overhaul', 4 May 2012.
[25] *Interfax*, 'Dve rossiyskiye atomnyye podlodki ispytayut oruzhiye v Norvezhskom more' ['Two Russian Submarines Set to Undergo Tests in the

Figure 6: *Yasen-M*-Class SSGN Under Construction at the Sevmash Yard in Severodvinsk on 18 April 2021

Source: Maxar Technologies and authors'

Figure 7: *Kilo*-Class Submarines at the Polyarny Naval Base on 1 May 2021

Source: Airbus Defence and Space and authors'

Table 1: The Submarines of Russia's Northern and Pacific Fleets

Class	Number of Boats in Fleet	Number Believed Active	Comments
Northern Fleet			
SSN/SSGN			
Sierra II	2	2	Recent refits may have enabled one or both of the submarines to be armed with Kalibr missiles
Victor III	3	2	B-448 *Tambov* in refit B-414 *Daniil Moskovsky* to be retired this year
Akula	3	0	Undergoing refits which will likely include being fitted with the Kalibr. Expected in service in the mid-2020s
Improved Akula	4	2	
Yasen/Yasen-M	2	2	
Oscar I, II	3	3	
SSK			
Kilo	5	5	
SSBN			
Delta	7	7	
Borei	1	1	
Pacific Fleet			
Oscar I, II	5	3	Two SSGNs in refit to carry 3M-54 Kalibr
Yasen	1	0	The *Novosirbirsk*, a *Yasen*-class on sea trials with the Pacific Fleet
Akula I, II	5	1	
Kilo	7	7	
Improved Kilo	2	2	Four more Project 636.3 submarines to be delivered by 2024
Borei	3	3	

Source: Author generated

Northern Sea'], 26 August 2019; Thomas Nilsen, 'Old Nuclear Sub Gets New Life at Nerpa Shipyard', *Barents Observer*, 5 October 2020; Franz-Stefan Gady, 'Russia's Pacific Fleet to Get Four Upgraded Nuclear Subs With Supersonic Cruise Missiles by 2021', *The Diplomat*, 7 February 2018; *Tass*, 'Russian Shipyard Floats Out Nuclear-Powered Akula-Class Sub After Upgrade', 26 December 2020. Office of Naval Intelligence, 'The People's Liberation Army Navy: A Modern Navy with Chinese Characteristics', August 2009; Amit Ray, 'Considerations and Challenges in Silencing Submarines', Indian Navy, <https://indiannavy.nic.in/insshivaji/sites/default/files/paper_on_considerations_and_challenges_in_silencing_submarines.pdf>, accessed 20 March 2021; Eugene Miasinkov, 'The Future of Russia's Strategic Nuclear Forces: Discussions and Arguments', Center for Arms Control, Energy and Environmental Studies', <http://armscontrol.ru/subs/snf/snf0322.htm>, accessed 12 February 2021; on methodological considerations when estimating submarine noise levels in open source, see also Wu Riqiang, 'Survivability of China's Sea-Based Nuclear Forces', *Science & Global Security* (Vol. 19, No. 2, 2011), pp. 91–121. Averaging results from multiple sources can allow for random errors to be

Table 2: The Approximate Noise Level at Source of Russian Submarines (Decibels)

Improved Los Angeles (Benchmark Western Submarine)	105 db
Akula	110 db
Improved Akula	100 db
Yasen	95 db
Victor II	120 db
Sierra	110 db
Kilo	110 db
Improved Kilo	105 db

Source: Author generated

Note: A submarine's noise level at source is the intensity of noise at 1 metre from the source. The noise level is divided into high-frequency (1khz band) continuous noise and low-frequency (5–200hz) discrete noise generation. The latter, being particularly salient for detection, is the subject of this table. The assumed speed of travel is 10 knots, though SSNs will exceed this speed in transit. It is also worth noting that decibels do not scale linearly. Thus, for example, a 5db difference in decibel levels means that one submarine is five times louder than the other.

The estimates arrived at by the academic literature surveyed by the authors about known noise profiles of submarines and relative noise differences – which can be used as benchmarks for estimates – are likely to be inaccurate given the secrecy which surrounds this data. However, as long as the *relative* comparisons between SSNs are accurate, this can still be the basis for modelling proportional capabilities. This stems from the fact that second-order tests, which examine the comparative differences between two entities, can be an accurate measure of distance so long as the error of the first-order test is systematic and not random. Nassim Nicholas Taleb and colleagues explains this phenomenon by way of an analogy in which a flawed tape- measure is used to measure the growth of two children. Even if the measure is incorrect, it will be a good approximation of the relative changes in their respective heights as well as being an accurate comparison between the two.[26] Assuming a broad accuracy in the proportional comparisons of Russian and Western SSNs, therefore, one can meaningfully examine their relative quietness and thus capabilities in a campaign. This will serve as a guiding assumption for the modelling later in this chapter.

---

disregarded in aggregate, though sources of inaccuracy – such as the systematic use of ONI reports by nearly all the literature surveyed – are likely to stay. The sources describing Chinese and Indian assets use Russian submarines as the baseline for comparisons.

[26] Nassim Nicholas Taleb et al., 'A New Heuristic Measure of Fragility and Tail Risks: Application to Stress Testing', International Monetary Fund Working Paper, WP/12/216, August 2012, p. 2.

Anti-Submarine Warfare

Russia's capacity for ASW is somewhat limited. Like its Soviet predecessor, the Russian navy aims for zonal area denial using a combination of airborne assets, submarines and surface vessels in a layered subsurface defensive system.[27] In addition to its submarines, the navy is likely to rely on maritime patrol aircraft such as the IL-38N and TU-142, as well as approximately 30 ASW-capable helicopters, including the Ka-27, Ka-28 and Ka-31 based out of Severomorsk-1.[28] While Russia has a broad range of ASW capable assets, its ability to coordinate them effectively is open to question.[29] Given that many of these assets are legacy Soviet assets, and that the USSR's navy struggled with coordination of ASW assets, it is conceivable that this remains an issue.[30] Indeed, Russian sensor capabilities have not kept up with improvements in quieting for submarines. That said, the OSK Sever does maintain the ability to effect a certain degree of coordination among its assets.

GUGI has expended significant amounts of effort over the past few years, placing underwater sensors and communications relays.[31] It has started placing Autonomous Nuclear Turbine Generator (ATGU) undersea power plants in parts of the Arctic shelf, likely in order to provide the power for a series of sonobuoy arrays. The Russians have also placed the MGK-608M Sever sensor system in the Barents Sea, replacing the older MGK-608.[32] These systems can communicate with ground stations up to 200 km away, meaning that they will likely be linked by fibre optic cables to Russia's new facilities on Kotelny, Alexandra Land and Wrangel, as well as being linked to the Kola Peninsula.[33] Satellites are another possible means of information relay, which might involve reliance on control and communications infrastructure outside the Northern Joint Command, where the authors could identify no space-related infrastructure. The coordination of ASW assets would likely be managed by the Northern Fleet's communications and electronic warfare (EW) centre at Severomorsk.

---

[27] On Soviet ASW, see Milan Vego, 'Submarines in Soviet ASW Doctrine and Tactics', *Naval War College Review* (Vol. 36, No. 2, 1983), pp. 2–15.

[28] Author imaging of Severomorsk-1.

[29] Author interview with retired Royal Navy ASW operator, London, 5 May 2021.

[30] Milan Vego, 'A World of Difference: Soviet Antisubmarine Warfare in 1991', *Naval War College Review* (Vol. 45, No. 3, 1992), pp. 58–77.

[31] H I Sutton, 'Analysis: Russia Seeks Submarine Advantage in the Arctic', *Covert Shores*, 20 September 2016.

[32] *Global Security*, 'Garmoniya/Harmony: RUSOSUS', <https://www.globalsecurity.org/intell/world/russia/harmony.htm>, accessed 10 May 2021.

[33] On the systems, see Sutton, 'Analysis: Russia Seeks Submarine Advantage in the Arctic'.

Russia maintains a significant network of SIGINT and EW facilities in the Arctic, which could be of use for ASW and also the disruption of an opponent's efforts to conduct such warfare in adjacent regions. The authors identified several sites as being of particular interest. Severomorsk Port, with its EW centre, is of particular importance. The port houses the 186th independent EW centre, which controls the long-range Murmansk BN EW system. This system would likely interfere with maritime communications over parts of the Barents Sea.[34] The authors also identified preliminary, though not conclusive, evidence of the exact location of the 186th's separate EW centre within Severomorsk. The 471st and 474th independent EW centres were also identified, with high confidence, at Kamchatka and Primorksy Krai, respectively.[35]

The conduct of a Russian ASW campaign in the Arctic would involve surface vessels. But, unlike its Soviet predecessor, the modern Russian navy has far fewer surface vessels for ASW operations. The Northern Fleet's two largest vessels, the *Kirov-* and *Slava*-class cruisers, both carry hull-mounted and variable depth sonar (VDS). The *Kirov* can carry three KA-27s while the *Slava* can carry one.[36] The *Sovremenny*-class destroyer has a more limited sonar capability, but can deploy a Ka-27.[37] It was originally intended to operate in tandem with *Udaloy II*-class ASW destroyers, of which there are two in the Northern Fleet. The *Udaloy*, in addition to possessing a more modern Zvezda M-2 sonar suite, has a standoff engagement capability against submarines in the form of the SS-N-14 anti-submarine missile.[38]

In addition to its larger warships, the fleet possesses a number of ASW-capable frigates and corvettes. Its modern *Gorshkov*-class frigates carry a towed-array sonar. This is an improvement over previous designs, which relied on hull-mounted sonar.[39] The four *Grisha III*-class corvettes in Severodvinsk, though far less capable than the *Gorshkov*, can also contribute to ASW.[40] Finally, the special purpose ships and submarines of the GUGI could, in principle, contribute to an ASW campaign. But the command and

---

[34] Thomas Nielsen, 'Russia Exercises Long-Range Radio-Electronic Warfare on Kola', *Barents Observer*, 4 November 2020.
[35] Author OSINT analysis – details in Appendix 2.
[36] *Naval Technology*, 'The Slava Class Guided Missile Cruiser', <https://www.naval-technology.com/projects/slavaclassguidedmiss/>, accessed 25 March 2021.
[37] Yves-Heng Lim, *China's Naval Power: An Offensive Realist Approach* (Farnham: Ashgate Publishing, 2014), p. 134.
[38] Eric Wertheim, 'Modernizing Udaloy-Class ASW Destroyers', *USNI Proceedings* (Vol. 146, No, 9, September 2020).
[39] *Navyrecognition*, 'Russia Laid Down Two Gorshkov-Class Frigates of Project 22350', April 2019.
[40] *RussianShips*, 'Small Anti-Submarine Ships', <http://russianships.info/eng/warships/project_1124.htm>, accessed 9 November 2021.

communication structures linking the GUGI to the navy are unclear – and may not exist given organisational stovepiping within Russia. The Pacific Fleet's surface ASW force is comprised entirely of *Grisha*-class corvettes.[41]

Even more pressing than limitations on its surface ASW assets, however, is Russia's lack of maritime patrol aircraft. The chief of the navy recently claimed that 30 IL-38s were active and were due to be upgraded to the more capable IL-38N.[42] It is likely that this number is an exaggeration – and that Russia fields approximately 16 IL-38 and IL-38N airframes.[43] Some of the IL-38Ns are based at Severomorsk-1, as well as the 317th Independent Air Regiment in Kamchatka. The Northern Fleet also has around 8 TU-142 MPAs, primarily under the aegis of the 3rd long-range anti-submarine aviation squadron based out of Fedotovo, with a further eight as part of the Pacific Fleet.[44]

It is worth noting, however, that Russian ASW operations can potentially at least partially offset the small number of available planes by shortening the flight times of IL-38Ns to Arctic operating zones. The construction and expansion of several facilities capable of hosting these planes could allow aircraft longer loiter times over parts of the Arctic and a level of access to friendly bases not enjoyed by hostile assets.

Perhaps most notably, Russian sensors and efforts to join them up have not improved substantially over the past few decades. Many Russian surface vessels use outdated sonar and the ability of platforms to share information is still limited. This is slowly changing, but remains a significant limitation on Russian ASW.

---

[41] *Kommersant,* 'The Entire Russian Fleet', 21 March 2021, <http://www.admiraltytrilogy.com/read/OOB_of_The_Russian_Fleet.pdf>, accessed 28 November 2021.

[42] *Navyrecognition,* 'Russian Navy to Receive About 30 Upgraded IL-38 Maritime Patrol Aircraft', <http://www.navyrecognition.com/index.php/news/defence-news/2017/february-2017-navy-naval-forces-defense-industry-technology-maritime-security-global-news/4873-russian-navy-to-receive-about-30-upgraded-il-38-maritime-patrol-aircraft.html>, accessed 9 November 2021; Michael Kofman, 'Russian Maritime "A2AD" Strengths and Weaknesses', Russian Military Analysis, 29 January 2020, <https://russianmilitaryanalysis.wordpress.com/2020/01/29/russian-maritime-a2-ad-strengths-and-weaknesses/>, accessed 28 November 2021.

[43] *BMPD Journal,* 'Na Severnom flote vosstanovleny dva aviatsionnykh polka' ['Two Naval Aviation Regiments Restored to the Northern Fleet'], 3 December 2019, <https://bmpd.livejournal.com/3860313.html>, accessed 10 May 2021; Westerlund and Oxenstierna (eds), *Russian Military Capability in a Ten-Year Perspective- 2019,* p. 71.

[44] Westerlund and Oxenstierna (eds), *Russian Military Capability in a Ten-Year Perspective- 2019,* p. 71.

Figure 8: IL-38 MPAs at Severomorsk-1

Source: Airbus Defence and Space and authors'

So, Russia enjoys a patchy but improving level of control under the Arctic seas. Improvements notwithstanding, however, the Russian navy will still struggle to effect denial against quiet Western SSNs in this region.

NATO

In many ways, NATO's deficiencies in this area match Russia's. While on paper NATO fields a formidable array of both subsurface and ASW assets, the whole is likely to be less than the sum of its parts. NATO's mobilisation for a high-intensity conflict would be in three phases under the aegis of a gradual response plan. The first, occurring within a week, entails the deployment of the assets committed to NATO's Very High Readiness Joint Task Force, including those of NATO's Standing Maritime Groups.[45] The

---

[45] The Very High Readiness Joint Task Force (VJTF) comprises the first part of a NATO response force to be mobilised at short notice. It is comprised of land, sea and air assets which can be mobilised in 48–72 hours. This includes a land brigade and elements from the two NATO Standing Maritime Groups, each comprised of four to six destroyers and frigates. See 'NATO, NATO Response Force', 20 September 2021, <https://www.nato.int/cps/en/natohq/49755.htm>, accessed 22 November 2021.

Figure 9: Russia's Arctic Airfields Capable of Hosting MPAs

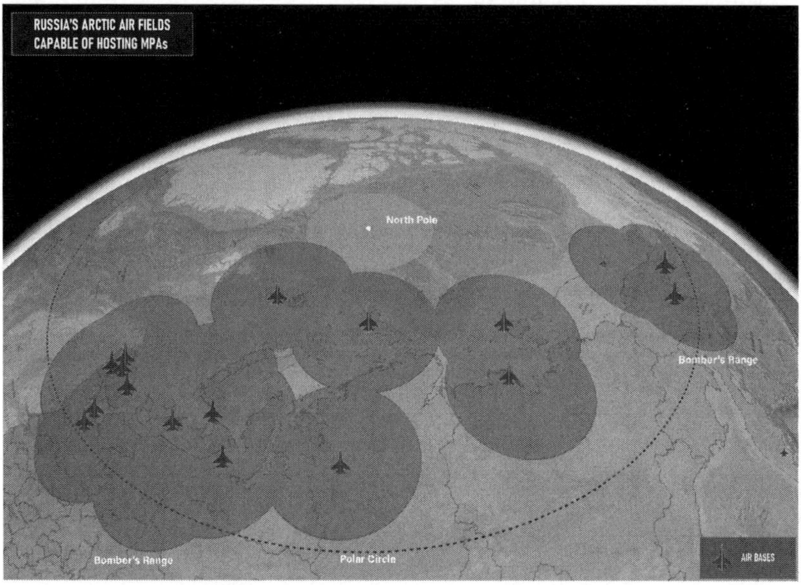

Source: Author generated

second phase of a Graduated Response Plan (GRP) entails a month to build up to the 'four 30s' – 30 combat vessels, 30 battalions, and 30 aircraft squadrons in 30 days.[46] Finally, follow-on forces under the aegis of the NATO Response Force would mobilise over a longer time period.[47] We assume that unless NATO can either prevail or at least contain Russian assets, follow-on forces are irrelevant. And, by extension, the balance of power in the earlier stages of a conflict is the most vital, with exercises such as *Dynamic Mongoose* being used as the basis for determining the proportion of ASW assets that could be mobilised within a relatively short time.[48] Longer-term exercises, such as *Trident Juncture* would suggest a larger force of NATO vessels being deployed to the High North – *Trident Juncture* involved 65 vessels, including 24 surface combatants. However,

---

[46] NATO, 'Press Conference by NATO Secretary General Jens Stoltenberg', 24 October 2019, <https://www.nato.int/cps/en/natohq/opinions_169936.htm>, accessed 22 November 2021.

[47] The NATO Response Force is a multinational joint force including both the VJTF and follow-on elements. See NATO, 'NATO Response Force'.

[48] *Dynamic Mongoose* involved five ships and five SSNs drawn primarily from NATO's Standing Maritime Group North, see *Naval Technology*, 'NATO Begins *Dynamic Mongoose 2020* Anti-Submarine Warfare Exercise', 30 June 2020.

two factors lead to a limit the authors' study of such a force ratio. First, *Trident Juncture* took several months to prepare. And, given that the median duration of a militarised crisis is 70 days (including the kinetic conflict period), it is likely irrelevant in an ASW battle. Even assuming offensive intent on NATO's part, one would need to assume Russian passivity in this build-up, which is unlikely. It is therefore the forces available at the outset of a conflict that are most important. The forces of NATO's standing maritime groups (SNMGs) and the assets at high readiness and very high readiness under the NATO Readiness Initiative are assessed to be of greatest salience. This paper treats NATO assets as being at 50% readiness at the outset of a conflict, reaching 70% within a month. It assesses Russian assets as being at 80% readiness due to the fact that the Northern Fleet is operating in its own backyard. These numbers are broadly reflective of the assumptions underpinning previous studies.[49]

The primary forward deployed component of the US naval commitment to Europe is four *Arleigh Burke*-class destroyers based at Rota, in Spain, and four P-8A Orions at Sigonella, in Sicily. While the primary purpose of the *Arleigh Burkes* is their contributions to the ballistic missile defence (BMD) system envisioned as part of the European Phased Adaptive Approach, the vessels are ASW capable.[50] *Arleigh Burkes* are equipped with the AN/SQR-19 towed-array sonar, as well as the AN/SQS-53C hull-mounted sonar.[51] It is, however, an open question whether any of these vessels will be diverted from their primary mission of BMD in an Arctic scenario.

The reconstitution of the US Navy's Second Fleet,[52] and a series of recent visits to northern waters by assets such as the *Seawolf*-class submarine, suggest that the US will maintain a larger number of assets engaged in the northern theatre of the European region in the future. At present, if it is correct to assume that the US will strive to maintain 60% of its SSN fleet in the Indo-Pacific at any given time, this would leave approximately 21 out of the remaining 51 vessels available for deployment.[53] If one assumes a high

---

[49] See, for example, Douglas Barrie et al., 'Defending Europe: Scenario-Based Capability Requirements for NATO's European Members', International Institute of Strategic Studies, April 2019, p. 20; Björn Ottosson, 'United States', in Eva Hagstöm Frisell and Krister Pallin (eds), *Western Military Capability in Northern Europe 2020: Part II National Capabilities* (Stockholm: FOI, 2021).

[50] Ottosson, 'United States', in Eva Hagstöm Frisell and Krister Pallin (eds), *Western Military Capability in Northern Europe 2020: Part II National Capabilities* (Stockholm: FOI, 2021).

[51] Federation of American Scientists, 'DDG-51 Arleigh Burke Class', <https://fas.org/man/dod-101/sys/ship/ddg-51.htm>, accessed 12 March 2021.

[52] *BBC*, 'U Resurrects Second Fleet to Counter Russia', 5 May 2018.

[53] Ben Werner, 'Indo-Pacom Commander Says Only Half of Sub Requests Are Met', *USNI News*, 27 March 2019.

peacetime readiness rate of 80% of the fleet being at – or close to – readiness, this implies that 16 vessels would in theory be available for deployment to northern European waters. Following work done by other analysts on the subject of rapid redeployment, we assume a baseline of 50% of vessels capable of redeploying in the early stages of a conflict, which would imply that approximately eight submarines could rapidly redeploy to Europe in the first week of a conflict – though fewer than this may be deployed, given the existence of other missions beyond great power competition.[54] On the other hand, given a month to build up assets in the region, it can be assumed that 13 SSNs – 70% of the available force – could be deployed to NATO's northern flank. Similarly, one might expect to see an initially limited number of surface combatants reallocated to northern Europe in a crisis, with institutions such as Sweden's FOI placing the number at four to seven in a week. Not all US surface assets deployed to Europe in a crisis involving Russia will be allocated to the High North. Missions in the Baltic Sea and the Atlantic will also likely take up resources. The authors assume, therefore, that half the available assets will be allocated to High North missions.[55]

For the purpose of this analysis, the authors assume that allied fleets such as the Royal Navy and the French navy are likely to be able to contribute a maximum of three ASW-optimised frigates apiece in the first weeks of a crisis and up to six after 30 days.[56] Currently, the Royal Navy would likely deploy its Type-23 frigate, though the arrival of the more modern Type-26 as a replacement is imminent. While the Royal Navy expects to field 12 frigates (FFGs), including eight Type-26s by the late 2020s, the demands of force protection for the UK's carrier battle groups are likely to compete with other missions.[57] The French navy maintains a similar force, though in any crisis involving Russia it may well see Mediterranean security as a competing priority, given the activity of the Black Sea fleet in this area.[58] It is assumed that Allies such as Germany and Italy would allocate their ASW-capable vessels closer to home in regions such as the Baltic Sea and Mediterranean in any conflict involving Russia. The Royal Navy has three *Astute*-class SSNs in active service, with another four entering service in the 2020s. It is assumed that the Royal Navy can deploy between one and three SSNs to the Arctic at present, based on the

[54] Eva Hagström Frisell et al., *Western Military Capability in Northern Europe* (Stockholm: FOI, 2020), p. 87.
[55] Hagström Frisell et al., *Western Military Capability in Northern Europe*, p. 87.
[56] *Ibid.*
[57] Sidharth Kaushal, 'A Globally Postured Regional Navy', *RUSI Defence Systems*, 24 March 2021; Kate Tringham, 'Naval Group Delivers First FREMM Air-Defence Frigate to French Navy', *Janes*, 19 April 2021.
[58] Igor Delanoe, 'Russia's Black Sea Fleet: Toward a Multiregional Force', CNA, 5 June 2019.

force likely to be available to the service over the course of the 2020s, and up to five over a longer period.[59] Britain expects to deploy nine P-8 Poseidon MPAs, while France sends 18 Atlantique II planes. Assuming a readiness rate of 50%, and the division of French assets discussed earlier, it is estimated that roughly four to six MPAs are available from each state over the course of a week and a month, respectively.[60]

Regional navies such as the Belgian, Norwegian and Danish navies will likely be able to contribute one or two ASW-capable vessels and, in the case of Norway, one or two SSKs at short notice. The Royal Norwegian air force expects to deploy five Poseidons by the mid-2020s.[61] In addition NATO members Germany and Italy could contribute one or two MPAs – although their focus is likely to be on the Baltic Sea and the Mediterranean.

Non-European NATO members such as Canada can make substantial contributions in the context of the subsurface domain. The Royal Canadian Navy and Air Force have 12 *Halifax*-class frigates (to be replaced by the Type-26) and 14 CP-140 Aurora MPAs.[62] While the centrality of the Arctic to Canadian security would suggest a priority being placed on the allocation of vessels to the High North, it is difficult to specify precisely how many would be available and how this would be weighed against competing missions not related to the west of the region. Assuming an availability of 50% at short notice and 60% of available assets being allocated, the authors assume four vessels would be made available.

In the absence of access to classified data, these assumptions amount to rough approximations. But they are likely to be broadly accurate and useful for modelling the rough balance of power in the subsurface area.

While not insubstantial on paper, this force is, as discussed below, highly vulnerable to disruption if it adopts a reactive posture.

---

[59] A lack of Arctic specialisation may also hamper French submarine operations in the northern theatre. Author interview with retired Royal Navy ASW Operator, 12 May 2021, London.

[60] *RAF News*, 'Fourth RAF Poseidon MRA1 Maritime Patrol Aircraft Named', 2 November 2020; *NavalNews*, 'French Navy Receives Third Upgraded ATL2 Maritime Patrol Aircraft', 24 April 2020.; Naval Technology, 'Halifax Class Frigates', <https://www.naval-technology.com/projects/halifax/>, accessed 21 March 2021.

[61] Viktor Lundquist, 'Denmark', in Hagstöm Frisell and Pallin (eds), *Western Military Capability in Northern Europe 2020: Part II National Capabilities*, p. 20; Jakob Gustafsson, 'Norway', in Hagstöm Frisell and Pallin (eds), *Western Military Capability in Northern Europe 2020: Part II National Capabilities*, p. 27–33.

[62] *NavalNews*, 'Canada's CP-140 Aurora MPA Upgraded to Block IV Takes First Flight', 22 February 2020.

Table 3: NATO ASW Assets Available in High North and Arctic Contingencies Within 7 and 30 Days of a Conflict

ASW Capable Surface Vessels	15–19
Attack Submarines (both SSKs and SSNs)	14–24
Maritime Patrol Aircraft	14–22

Source: Author generated

Modelling Interactions Between NATO and Russian Forces in the High North

The authors considered three distinct scenarios in the context of the High North

1 Efforts to demonstrate capability in the context of a sub-threshold dispute (consistent with a moderate level of Russian ambition).
2 A Russian effort to break out of the High North in the context of a conflict with NATO (consistent with a high level of ambition).
3 NATO efforts to break into the region, both in the context of competition and warfighting (consistent with purely defensive Russian ambitions).

The last two scenarios reflect two plausible NATO concepts of operations: defensive sea control and a forward maritime posture. Each concept could support NATO's strategic objectives in the context of a conflict which began either in the High North or elsewhere. Defensive sea control starts from the assumption that the primary threat posed by Russian assets is their ability to threaten NATO SLOCs and critical infrastructure and that containment is vital. By contrast, offensive sea control would entail efforts to limit the Northern Fleet's freedom of action in its own area of control. As with the maritime strategy of the 1980s, this approach would mean treating Russia's northern flank as having asymmetrical vulnerability – possibly in order to offset Russian strengths in a conflict that started in another region.

Submarines have typically not been seen as a presence force capable of tasks such as deterrent signalling. However, the ability to effectively track an opponent's submarines has shaped perceptions of the balance of power in previous competitions, such as the Third Battle of the Atlantic between US and Soviet submarines.[63] The authors therefore assume that in the context of a sub-threshold competition in the context of a Russian effort to dominate the NSR in peacetime, demonstrating a force's capacity for

---

[63] For an example of the view that submarines are of limited use as a peacetime competitive tool, see Erik Gartzke and Jon Lindsay, 'The Influence of Sea Power on Politics: Domain- and Platform-Specific Attributes of Material Capabilities', *Security Studies* (Vol. 29, No. 4, October 2020), pp. 601–36.

counter-detection of hostile submarines will be crucial to establishing in an opponent's mind the ability to control the region or dispute control in wartime.[64] Submarines may be a less visible presence asset than surface vessels, but the authors contend that their role in deterrence and signalling has been somewhat understated.

In the context of a high-intensity conflict – which has not necessarily been launched in the Arctic – the authors consider two scenarios. First, a scenario in which the Russian Northern Fleet's submarines, potentially reinforced by assets from the Pacific Fleet, attempt to break out from bases in the Barents Sea. This could imply a limited sortie through Norwegian waters to threaten European ports as well as create new threat vectors in a precision strike campaign by using submarine-launched cruise missiles (SLCMs) to target critical assets, such as tanker aircraft or ships in port.[65] A more ambitious plan might see some Russian assets attempt to breach the GIUK Gap in a bid to target critical infrastructure such as transatlantic sea cables.

The second scenario is a NATO effort to break into the Arctic in a way envisaged by Reagan-era maritime strategy. While there is no indication that this is NATO policy, there are in theory conceivable reasons why the Alliance might opt for such an approach.[66] For example, asymmetrical retaliation might be deemed a cost-effective means of deterring a Russia that is dominant on land. A threat to the critical infrastructure of the Russian Arctic and one leg of Russia's nuclear triad could compel Moscow to de-escalate, irrespective of the balance of power on the ground – though the escalatory risks of such an approach have been the subject of some debate.[67] Neutralising surface vessels and subsurface assets conducting a conventional precision strike campaign within the context of a European conflict might be deemed desirable. One might also consider the 'nightmare scenario' (from a Russian perspective) – NATO submarines infiltrating the Arctic to conduct a precision strike campaign exploiting a weak spot in radar coverage.[68] This could target Russian early-warning systems and air-defence assets such as the MIG-

---

[64] Cote Jr, *The Third Battle*.
[65] On the threat posed by SLCMs, see Daryl Press's presentation at the 2020 RUSI Space and Missile Defence Conference, 27 February 2020.
[66] On the Reagan administration's Maritime Strategy, see Peter Swartz and John Hattendorf (eds), *US Naval Strategy in the 1980s: Selected Documents* (Newport, RI: Naval War College, 2008).
[67] For a useful overview of this debate, see Steven E Miller and Stephen Van Evera (eds), *Naval Strategy and National Security* (Princeton, NJ: Princeton University Press, 1988).
[68] Kofman, speech at RUSI Seapower Conference.

31BM in their air bases as well as communications, critical national infrastructure and economic assets.[69]

It is worth reiterating that the purpose of this paper is not to assess policy but the level of ambition that existing Russian and NATO assets can support. The authors can therefore make no claims as to the levels of aggression expected from either party.

In order to assess the relative balance of forces, the authors have relied on a series of quasi-deterministic search models.[70] Such models can approximate the interplay of key variables in military interactions, though they are by no means perfect predictors – their results should be taken as a first cut to inform subsequent analysis. The authors made a series of stylised assumptions about the search methods used. For example, ASW assets and submarines relied entirely on passive detection (a not entirely unrealistic assumption, given that active detection is used sparingly because of the risks it entails).

The relative detection ranges of Russian and NATO submarines is worked out through the passive sonar equation $TL=DT+NL-AG-SL$,[71] where SL is the noise at source, AG is the array gain, NL is the ambient noise level, and TL is the transmission loss. The range at which a submarine can be detected is a function of the acceptable transmission loss – that is, $DT+NL-AG-SL$. Transmission losses are proportional to distance given by $20 .Log_{10}d$. Transmission losses are a function of a number of factors, including water depth and the depth of the mixed layer.[72] As a rule, transmission losses increase in Arctic climates due to higher absorption and greater surface reflection. The varying depth and ambient noise levels of the individual seas which, collectively, make up the Arctic and High North are another source of transmission loss. In the Norwegian and Barents Seas, these losses average 77 db and 72 db respectively.[73] As a cookie-cutter assumption, the authors

---

[69] On Russian fears regarding such an attack, see Dave Johnson, 'Russia's Conventional Precision Strike Capabilities, Regional Crises, and Nuclear Thresholds', Livermore Papers on Global Security, 2018, pp. 20–30.

[70] While a stochastic model would have been preferable given the number of variables at play, this would have added to the complexity of the process to a degree that exceeded its value. Indeed, deterministic models have proved useful in operations analysis. See Alan Washburn and Moshe Kress, *Combat Modeling* (New York, NY: Springer, 2009).

[71] DT, the detection threshold for a submarine, is calculated on the basis of a detection index, the bandwidth frequency of the receiver and the time taken for integration. It is (5Log dw)/T. For further details, see Eugene Miasnikov, 'Can Russian Strategic Submarines Survive at Sea? The Fundamental Limits of Passive Acoustics', *Science & Global Security* (Vol. 4, No. 2, 1994), pp. 213–51.

[72] Miasnikov, 'Can Russian Strategic Submarines Survive at Sea?'

[73] William C Dixon and C Ray Rollins, 'Very Low Frequency Acoustic Detection of Submarines', Naval Research Laboratory, 1977; Øivind Grenness, 'Acoustic Ambient Noise in the Barents Sea', SACLANTCEN Conference Proceedings CP-32 (Vol. 2, Part 1, 1982), pp. 8–1 to 8–9.

Table 4: Detection Range by Different Sensors[74]

	Passive Detection by Towed-Array Sonar	Hull-Mounted Sonar Passive[75]	Retired ASW Operator Estimate (Passive Towed Array)[76]
Akula	7nm	<5nm	5nm
Improved Akula	4nm	4nm	3nm
Yasen	3nm	<3nm	1nm
Victor	15 nm	10nm	10 nm
Sierra	12nm	6nm	10 nm
Kilo	10nm	4nm	<1 nm
Improved Kilo	<5nm	<5 nm	<1 nm
Improved Los Angeles	10nm	4nm	3-10 nm
Seawolf	3 nm	<3nm	3-10 nm
Virginia	3nm	<3nm	5 nm
Astute[77]	3nm	<3nm	<5nm
Ula SSK	n/a[78]	n/a	n/a

Source: Author generated

assumed ambient noise levels of 70–90 db. Details of the modelling process can be found in the appendices.

The authors' estimates are relatively close to the lower bound estimates of the retired Royal Navy ASW practitioner, who contributed to this paper's findings, implying a degree of fidelity. They depart from it in some cases but are not systematically more optimistic for either ASW operators or submarines. Based on this rough set of estimates, the authors were able to run a series of search model based on the pioneering work of Alan Washburn. The models were Washburn's barrier search models and the exhaustive search model for scenarios in which effective cueing of one ASW asset by another was assumed.[79]

---

[74] All figures are at an assumed frequency of 50hz, with the speed of travel being 8 knots. The detection radius of a sonobuoy and a MAD were assumed at a standard of 6 km and 1600 m respectively. For fidelity, we also asked a retired Royal Navy ASW operator for range estimates.

[75] The array gains for hull-mounted sonar were assumed to be 10 db less than towed array – based on Miasnikov, 'Can Russian Strategic Submarines Survive at Sea?'. The authors also assumed that passive hull-mounted sonar will be used to avoid ASW vessels being targeted by SLCM-equipped submarines, which is a reasonable, but not perfectly realistic, assumption.

[76] All estimates are in the lower bound, which is accepted as an assumption due to climactic difficulties.

[77] The *Astute's* presumed noise level is benchmarked to the *Virginia*, because the two submarines share a number of characteristics, including pump jet propulsion.

[78] Benchmarked against the *Kilo* for modelling.

[79] For more details about the combat models used, see Washburn and Kress, *Combat Modeling*, Chapter 7.

In a conflict scenario, the authors modelled NATO defensive planning as mirroring its Cold War posture, with SSNs and mines forming a forward barrier at the Bear Island Norway gap and FFGs and maritime patrol aircraft operating at and ahead of the GIUK Gap. It is worth noting at the outset that this is not entirely descriptively accurate – given differences in hull numbers, SSNs are unlikely to be used in barrier detection as was the case during the Cold War. They are likely to be tasked with ASW after a target was identified and tracked by other assets. The barrier detection model can still serve as a proxy for sensor coverage in ASW. The effects of multi-static, low frequency detection, networking and sensor fidelity are also partially incorporated into the authors' modelling. The model used is an analytical abstraction comparable to the Forward Edge of the Battle Area (FEBA) model used in the analysis of ground operations as opposed to a perfect description of either side's tactics.

During the Cold War, it was assumed that ASW against the Soviet submarine fleet would involve five barriers, which submarines would need to transit twice to and from the Atlantic. Multiple SSN barriers were envisioned as being part of this strategy. So it is reasonable to estimate that more than 50 SSNs would have been needed on station.[80] By contrast, NATO would, under present circumstances, be able to erect two barriers. Indeed, the four-hour loiter time of MPAs without air-to-air refuelling means that in the absence of large numbers of tanker aircraft – which may be needed for other tasks – around one to two could be kept in the air to maintain 24-hour surveillance of the GIUK gap.[81] With tanker refuelling, the number of aircraft that can be kept in the air at one time will rise, though the degree to which this occurs depends on the availability of air-to-air refuelling. The authors vary the number of MPAs on station to between two and four. This is broadly realistic as human limitations would also demand daily aircraft rotations even when refuelling is available. Helicopters such as the MH-60R deployed on the *Arleigh Burkes* and the Merlin MK-1 and 2s, which can be flown from the Royal Navy's Type-23s, Type-26s and Type-45s, will also provide intermittent ASW coverage, albeit limited by their times on station.[82]

---

[80] Michael Kevin McMahon, 'Defending Norway and the Northern Flank: Analysis of NATO's Defensive Options', unpublished thesis, Naval Postgraduate School, 1985; Alain C Enthoven and K Wayne Smith, *How Much Is Enough? Shaping the Defence Program, 1961–69* (Santa Monica, CA: RAND, 1971), pp. 140–60; Barry Posen, *Inadvertent Escalation*, pp. 150–70.

[81] The 18-hour loiter time of French Atlantique aircraft partially offsets this limitation.

[82] Boeing, 'P-8: An Intelligence, Surveillance and Reconnaissance Solution', <https://www.boeing.com/defense/maritime-surveillance/p-8-poseidon/index.page#/tech-spec>, accessed 12 November 2021.

Although the Russian submarine fleet is smaller than its Soviet predecessor, it does have two advantages. First, it is unlikely that NATO will have enough submarines in the early days of a conflict to put up multiple barriers, as it would have had during the Cold War.[83] Second, if Russian plans which envision having to fight short, sharp conflicts are in fact correct, then the assumptions of the Cold War – for example, that Soviet submarines would have to run the gauntlet of NATO barriers multiple times to and from the Atlantic – are no longer true. A nuclear submarine can remain on station for the entirety of a 30–50-day conflict. Furthermore, many missions in the High North would require even less of Russian submariners. To strike northern European ports with Kalibr missiles, for example, they would only need to transit one barrier and launch missiles from positions well ahead of the GIUK Gap. In addition, the force conducting operations is considerably quieter than its Soviet predecessor.

NATO surface forces conducting barrier defence are vulnerable to Russia's long-range anti-surface warfare (ASuW) assets, such as long-range anti-ship cruise missiles on submarines. This is discussed in later chapters, but given the limited initial forces available to NATO, relatively small numbers of frigate losses, for example, could effectively rupture the Alliance's defensive posture in the GIUK Gap.

However, Russia has its own problems in this area. Its lack of MPAs, and a limited number of credible ASW-capable vessels equipped with towed-array sonar, significantly limit Russia's own defensive capabilities. Russia's MPAs, however, benefit from longer loiter times than NATO counterparts, which partially offsets force structure issues.[84] Russia also has ASW capable Ka-27, Ka-29 and Ka-31 helicopters in the area, operating from Severomorsk-1, though these are not optimal assets for wide-area defence. The fact that there are a number of routes of ingress into the Russian Arctic for submarines – unlike for surface vessels – represents a further complication as it means some assets will be spread thin. For example, the transpolar route into the Arctic has been crossed by US submarines for years – potentially allowing the bastion to be circumvented. Russian assets will therefore need to be spread across the region.[85] The question of how well

---

[83] UK Armed Forces Commentary, 'The Merlin Family in UK Service', 11 May 2011, <http://ukarmedforcescommentary.blogspot.com/2011/05/merlin-family-in-uk-service.html>, accessed 12 November 2021; Lockheed Martin, 'MH-60R', <https://www.lockheedmartin.com/en-us/products/sikorsky-mh-60-seahawk-helicopters.html>, accessed 12 November 2021.

[84] The IL-38N can stay on station for 12 hours, if operating from airfields such as Severomorsk-1 and 3, as can the TU-142. See Peter G Dancey, *Soviet Aircraft Industry* (Stroud: Fonthill Media, 2015).

[85] Waldo Lyon, *The Polar Submarine and Navigation of the Arctic Ocean* (San Diego, CA: US Navy Electronics Laboratory, 1959).

Table 5: Average Number of Engagement Opportunities for NATO and Russian Assets at Two Barriers in a 12-Hour Period Against Opponents' Quiet Submarines[86]

ASW System	Pd
Russian	0.055–0.06
NATO[87]	0.08–0.086

Source: Author generated

networked Russia's ASW assets are is another limitation. Its own fleet of SSNs and SSKs would struggle to form multiple barriers as well.

The authors assume that in the event Russian forces did sortie from the Arctic, they would be *Akula* and Severodvisk SSNs/SSGNSs because of their relative quietness, while older SSNs would join SSKs in defending the bastion. NATO barrier defence is assumed to be identical to the Cold War. By contrast, Russian assets are assumed to be divided between two missions. First, a layered bastion defence of SSNs, SSKs, surface vessels and MPAs is assumed to be put up in the Western portion of the region. However, the authors also assume that around 20% of Russian assets will be deployed to create a barrier defence in the Central Arctic. The authors primarily examine the dynamics in the Western Arctic, however, given the primacy of this theatre. The results of the authors' modelling are discussed below.

Both Russian and NATO submarines appear highly survivable, with the Alliance enjoying a marginal advantage. However, neither side has the ASW capability to deny the other's submarines the opportunity to do significant damage. It is worth noting that this model envisioned Russian submarines breaking past two ASW barriers – one off Norway and then the GIUK Gap. In reality, they may need only to penetrate the first, significantly improving their odds. On the other hand, the differences in performance of Russian sensors and processing systems could be incorporated only imperfectly, and the authors assume that the quietest Russian submarines will be able to slip out of the bastion. This means that part of this advantage may reflect limitations of the modelling process. The figures for barrier penetration are significantly more optimistic for submariners than was the case during the Cold War when, for example, the probability of detection of a submarine at a given barrier was assumed to be around 0.15 (15%).[88] As modern submarines are quieter and ASW capabilities on both sides have atrophied, a halving of each side's effectiveness as the authors' models suggest may well be accurate. However, this should be taken as an early finding to inform a subsequent, more granular analysis.

---

[87] Assuming a two-barrier defence – the Greenland Norway and GIUK Gaps.
[88] Posen, *Inadvertent Escalation*, p. 235.

Although both Russian and NATO ASW assets should get at least some cueing from each other, as well as systems such as SOSUS and HARMONY – even if they are not perfectly networked – the assumption of operating without cueing is worth considering. Random search models assume non-cueing, which may be reasonable given Russian difficulties in this area and the potential for NATO networking to be disrupted by a range of Russian activities. However, to incorporate asymmetries in networking into the authors' model, a discount rate of 0.3 is imposed on Russian Pd. This method has been used in other contexts to incorporate factors such as training and networking into a model without adding to its complexity.[89] While questions over the fidelity of the models are reasonable, their results track well with what one would expect when comparing the assets at play in the GIUK Gap currently with those available during the Cold War.[90]

Analysis

While submarines and anti-submarine capabilities will not be stand-alone assets for either NATO or Russia, and will be part of a wider maritime CONOPS, their effective use will be critical to both of the operational concepts that either Russia or NATO can pursue in the High North. Any effort by NATO to defend its members in the High North, as well as limit the Russian subsurface threat, will – at a minimum – require defensive sea control at chokepoints such as the GIUK and Bear Island Norway Gaps. By contrast, an approach that stresses offensive sea control and power projection against the Russian northern flank would rely on submarines to a significant degree. SSNs in forward positions could play a key role in eliminating the surface vessels that form the maritime component of Russia's integrated air-defence system. SSGNs, such as *Ohios*, and SSNs such as *Virginias* – equipped with the *Virginia* payload module – could conduct long-range strikes from forward positions against C4ISR[91] nodes in support of a joint air campaign. Finally, SSNs can menace Russia's SSBNs. Russia can use its SSNs and SSGNs either in a defensive role to protect its bastions or in an offensive capacity to eliminate surface vessels and conduct strikes against critical infrastructure in Europe. An aggressive approach in the early stages of a conflict when Russia enjoys some advantages could see NATO's ASW assets targeted and thereby open the way for Russian special purpose

---

[89] See, for example, Heginbotham et al., *The US–China Military Scorecard*, p. 350.
[90] For a useful Late Cold War study, see Posen, *Inadvertent Escalation*.
[91] Submarine Industrial Base Council, 'Virginia Payload Module', 2015, <http://submarinesuppliers.org/wp-content/uploads/2015/07/Virginia-Payload.pdf>, accessed 28 November 2021.

submarines to interfere with critical undersea infrastructure. While SSNs are unlikely to act as surface vessel hunters, given that they are few in number, they may be given this role if the operational rewards justify it.

What is most notable about the undersea balance is the fact that both Russia and NATO are operating from a position of relative insecurity. The number of engagement opportunities afforded to both Russian and NATO assets in the High North suggests that both are highly vulnerable on the defensive – but also have an incentive to push forward.

In the context of a grey-zone dispute, this could afford NATO both opportunities and hazards to both parties. On the one hand, should Russian SSNs and SSGNs escape their northern bastions in peacetime, they could pose the risk of pre-emption against key facilities, such as air bases and ports, should competition escalate to conflict. SSGNs such as the *Yasen*, which will have a special purpose, could also conduct a range of activities from intelligence gathering to threatening undersea cables.

NATO, aware of the challenges of ASW, could be incentivised to push into the Arctic to pin down Russian SSNs in the region. This is a particularly viable option given the limitations of Russia's ASW capabilities. This would certainly have the desired effect of forcing the reallocation of Russian SSNs, because even a full suite of SSKs and SSNs has a poor record according to the authors' models. This may even have a strong deterrent effect given Russia's congenital fear of a maritime precision strike campaign launched from its northern flank. On the cost side, however, it may prompt risky Russian behaviour on the basis of fear.

In a conflict scenario, as described above, both NATO and Russia will struggle to defend. For NATO, this means the risk of multiplying missile challenges and risks to assets such as undersea cables. For Russia, the traditional risk to its SSBN fleet is compounded by broader fears, as described above.

NATO could act creatively on this front, posturing aggressively in the Arctic to force de-escalation in a mirror of Russia's own 'escalate to de-escalate' concept for its own SSN forward deployment, or to force Russian SSNs to operate defensively.[92] If this is the case, more SSGNs and an additional emphasis on placing precision strike assets on existing SSNs could exacerbate Russian fears. This might be one way to counter Russian efforts to target the gaps in NATO's escalation ladder through calibrated 'assigned damage'. Alternatively, should this appear too risky, reinforcing NATO's ASW capability in the High North will prove critical.

---

[92] Dave Johnson, *Nuclear Weapons in Russia's Approach to Conflict* (Paris: FRS, 2016).

CHAPTER III: RUSSIAN AND NATO SURFACE CAPABILITIES IN THE HIGH NORTH

Key Points

- Russia's growing anti-access network, coupled with its capacity to maintain a persistent presence, gives it effective peacetime control over the NSR.
- In a conflict scenario, Russia's surface forces in the High North operating in tandem with air-based assets can inflict limited, but militarily significant, attrition on NATO assets in the Norwegian and Barents Seas.
- NATO fares better in conflict simulations when it opts for a pulsed forward-leaning maritime posture – in effect, sinking Russian ships in their bastions – as compared to when it attempts to contain the Northern Fleet. This is true despite a forward posture placing vessels closer to Russian defences.
- The balance of power on the surface may make it easier for Russian subsurface assets to break out of the GIUK Gap if the attrition suggested by this chapter against the NATO vessels manning it is achieved. This is only true if NATO adopts a reactive posture, however.

The balance of power on the ocean surface in the Arctic will have a crucial role in determining the relative capacity of NATO and Russia to exert influence in the region and the High North in both peacetime and war. This balance will be impacted by related factors such as the balance of power in the air and subsurface domain.

When discussing Russia's surface capabilities in the Arctic, the scope needs to extend beyond naval platforms. This stems from the symbiotic relationship between Russia's naval forces in the Arctic, its coast guard, and commercial assets such as its nuclear-powered icebreaker fleet. Indeed, the relationship between the security services and functions such as border security has always been relatively tight – the FSB, for example, is in charge of border security.[1] The assets held by the Russian border

---

[1] Thomas Nilsen, 'Russian Coast Guard Receives New Ice Strengthened Patrol Vessel', *Barents Observer*, 30 December 2019.

guard in the region, such as the Project 22100 *Okean*-class icebreaker which is equipped with a 76 mm gun and can carry a Ka-27 helicopter, are capable of enforcing the country's peacetime claims over the NSR. The Russian naval force structure in the region is increasingly embracing both presence and warfighting functions. For example, the Northern Fleet's new Project 23550 patrol icebreaker will combine the functions of an icebreaker and a warship and is equipped with a missile suite not typically seen on patrol vessels.[2]

In combination with Russia's icebreaker fleet – the world's largest and best equipped – a combination of coast guard and naval vessels could exert effective peacetime control over the NSR. This would be sufficient to enforce Russian laws such as prospective legislation that demands that vessels transiting the route use Russian pilots and icebreakers.[3]

In wartime, Russia's surface forces will operate in tandem with subsurface, ground and air strike assets to control the routes of ingress into the Arctic. The coastal defence forces of the Northern Fleet's joint command have been strengthened by the deployment of the Bastion-P coastal defence anti-ship system on islands, such as Kotelny and Alexandra Land.[4] The system is currently equipped with a 400 km range supersonic P-800 missile, though the adoption of the 800 km range P-800M is likely.[5] Notably, Russian commentators discuss cueing the Bastion-P using low observable Project 22160 patrol vessels.[6] While these vessels are not part of the Northern Fleet, this would suggest a role for smaller vessels and perhaps coast guard vessels as spotters.

The locations of the fleet's Bastion-P batteries is interesting. While the choice of Alexandra Land is unsurprising, as Bastion-P systems there can deny stretches of the Barents Sea, as well as the northern approaches to the Arctic from the Greenland Sea, it is unlikely that Allied surface vessels would be near Kotelny in wartime. Rather, these assets would appear to

---

[2] *Naval Technology*, 'Ivan Papanin (Project 23550) Class Arctic Patrol Vessels'. The vessels, which are Arctic rated, will be armed with the Kalibr-NK.

[3] Christopher Woody, 'As US Tries to Close "Icebreaker Gap" With Russia, Its Only Working Icebreaker Is Making a Rare Trip North', *Business Insider*, 9 November 2020.

[4] Identified by authors using open-source imagery.

[5] Charles Bartles, 'Improvements to the Onyx Coastal Defence Missile', OE Watch, December 2019, <https://community.apan.org/wg/tradoc-g2/fmso/m/oe-watch-articles-2-singular-format/345363.29/11/2021>, accessed 12 May 2021.

[6] Aleksey Ramm and Bogdan Stepovoy, 'S korablya na «Bastion»: ataka beregovykh batarey stanet vnezapnoy' ['From Ship to "Bastion": Shore Batteries Attack Will Be Sudden'], *Izvestiya*, 22 October 2019, <https://iz.ru/930452/aleksei-rammbogdan-stepovoi/s-korablia-na-bastion-ataka-beregovykh-batarei-stanet-vnezapnoi>, accessed 29 November 2021.

make more sense in the context of peacetime competition – forcing any vessel operating within Russia's claimed territories to do so under the shadow of an anti-access area denial (A2/AD) system. The option to escalate on favourable terms lends credibility to peacetime blackmail and coercion – a dynamic observed in the South China Sea. The presence of Chinese anti-ship missiles – even if they remain unused – precludes nations like Vietnam and the Philipines from using their navies to push back against encroachments by China's navy and coast guard. A similar rationale may guide the emplacement of the Bastion-P on Kotelny, which could allow Russia to set the tempo of escalation in any competition over the status of the NSR.[7]

Additionally, the air-based strike capabilities held by the Northern Fleet have seen a qualitative improvement – the KH-47M2 Kinzhal quasi-ballistic missile and the KH-32 cruise missile have been fielded both on strategic bombers and, in the case of the former, on the MIG-31 K.[8] The ability of subsurface assets such as the *Oscar II* and *Yasen* to launch the supersonic P-800 Oniks and hypersonic Zircon cruise missiles will render these assets increasingly lethal at long ranges.[9]

The layered defensive system that Russia hopes to put in place could serve to constrain the activities of other states' surface forces in both peacetime and in war. However, the effectiveness of this system will depend, in no small part, on Russia's ability to both sustain a forward regional presence based on its Arctic infrastructure and on its ability to coordinate a range of reconnaissance assets from satellites to maritime patrol aircraft to deliver situational awareness to assets which are constrained more by their organic sensors than by the effective ranges of the strike capabilities they field.

In principle, this force could serve a number of roles. Analysts such as Michael Kofman have noted that in many ways damage limitation as opposed to A2/AD might best characterise Russia's maritime strategy with the emphasis being on mitigating the effects of NATO's superiority at sea as opposed to denying stretches of sea space.[10] While this is plausible, it might be worth considering that in due course the emergent Arctic force

---

[7] On China see Bryan Clark, Mark Gunzinger and Jesse Sloman, 'Winning in the Gray Zone: Using Electromagnetic Warfare to Regain Escalation Dominance', Center for Strategic and Budgetary Assessments, 2017, p. 18.

[8] *Militarywatch Magazine*, 'Russia's Lethal New Kinzhal "Carrier Killer" Hypersonic Missile Set to Bring Renewed Foreign Interest in MiG-31 and Tu-22M as Launch Platforms for Maritime Strike Roles', 3 August 2018.

[9] H I Sutton, 'Powerful Russian Submarine Seen Entering Baltic Sea', *Forbes*, 10 July 2020.; Ryan White, 'The 1st Launch of the Hypersonic "Zircon" from a Sub to be Performed Not Earlier Than June', *Naval Post*, 4 March 2021.

[10] Kofman, speech given at RUSI Sea Power Conference.

Figure 10A: Russia's Improving Sea Denial Network – Bastion-P TELS on Kotelny Island

Source: Maxar Technologies and authors'

Figure 10B: Russia's Improving Sea Denial Network – Bastion-P TELS on Alexandra Land

Source: Maxar Technologies and authors'

structure can sustain a more ambitious approach. Under this approach, Russian assets in the region can assert localised sea control over key stretches of the NSR, as well as adjoining seas such as the Barents and Norwegian Seas. In line with the rest of the paper, this chapter examines the scope of ambition that the emerging Russian regional force structure can underpin without making claims as to the level of ambition entertained by Moscow.

The Surface Capabilities and Supporting Infrastructure of the Northern Fleet

For the purposes of this chapter, surface capabilities will include all assets relevant to the control of the ocean surface, including ground-based missiles, submarines and aerial strike assets. The Russian approach to surface warfare is in many ways an evolution of the Soviet Union's strategy of erecting layered defences around the country's coastlines. In the event of a conflict, long-range strategic bombers would form the outer layer of this defensive system, followed by SSNs and SSGNs. The final layer of the defensive system would be Russia's surface forces and its shorter-ranged diesel-electric submarines. In effect, this amounts to a sequential model of attack in which an opponent such as a US carrier strike group would be faced with increasingly dense missile salvos as it moved into position through a layered defence.

Contemporary Russian discussions of maritime competition tend to assume a role for surface assets in a strategic continental operation, where naval assets play a role in the defence of coastlines critical to the conduct of land operations. Alternatively, they are discussed in a strategic oceanic theatre of operations, where Russian assets at sea, on land and in the air have the aims of defending key coastlines, defeating an opponent's major naval formations and destroying coastal targets.[11] It is worth noting that naval assets also have a role in strategic aerospace operations. These assets will conduct precision strikes at depth against land targets as well as nuclear operations where the range of tactical and strategic nuclear assets held by the Russian navy come into play as a means of either de-escalating on Russian terms or engaging in nuclear exchanges.[12] As such, uniquely among Russian services, the navy has a role across the spectrum of strategic operations, for which assets held in

---

[11]   Office of Naval Intelligence, 'The Russian Navy: A Historic Transition', December 2015, p. 3; Johnson, 'Russia's Conventional Precision Strike Capabilities, Regional Crises, and Nuclear Thresholds', p. 33.

[12]   Johnson, 'Russia's Conventional Precision Strike Capabilities, Regional Crises, and Nuclear Thresholds', p. 33.

the Arctic will be crucial. At a minimum, then, Russia's surface control assets in the Arctic will be expected to make the presence of adversary surface vessels along the NSR difficult in wartime. They may also be able to make it difficult for forces in the Bear Island–Norway and GIUK Gaps and help subsurface assets escape into the Atlantic. But as the tasks of ASW and ASuW will draw on many of the same assets, this will limit the capabilities Russian commanders will have to allocate to each function at any given time.

Although surface vessels of the Northern Fleet are capable, they are in many cases ageing. The fleet's *Kirov* cruisers – its largest vessels – are equipped with the P-700 Granit anti-ship cruise missile, which will be replaced with the P-800, and are defended by a maritime version of the S-300 SAMs. The vessels sensors include the long-range MR-800 Voshkod radar, the MR-710 and the MR320 air- and surface-search radars. These systems are older analogue radars which operate in the S-band.[13] Their effective passive detection range against a surface target is likely to be in the range of 300 km in passive search and 150 km in active search.[14] Though limited in terms of its capacity for surface detection, the *Kirov* also carries up to three Ka-27 helicopters, extending its situational awareness further out. It also has point defences, including 64 3K95 and 40 SA-N-4 short-range SAMs, as well as the AK-630 and a Close In Weapons System (CIWS).

The fleet's newest surface combatants, its *Gorshkov*-class frigates, have 16 USK VLS cells, which are capable of launching the 3M54 Kalibr as well as the P-800 Oniks and, when introduced, the Zircon.[15] The vessels are equipped with a Monolit 3K41 over-the-horizon (OTH) radar, which has a passive detection range of 400 km and an active detection range of 250 km.[16] The vessels possess a CIWS.

Older vessels such as the *Sovremenny*- and *Slava*-classes, provide capability to varying degrees. The *Sovremenny*, equipped with the Mineral ME OTH radar system and the supersonic Moskit ASCM, is still a

---

[13] Analogue radars are in general more vulnerable to jamming, see Justin Bronk, 'Modern Russian and Chinese Integrated Air Defence Systems: The Nature of the Threat, Growth Trajectory and Western Options', *RUSI Occasional Papers* (April 2021).

[14] Norman Friedman, *The Naval Institute Guide to World Naval Weapon Systems*, 5th ed. (Annapolis, MD: Naval Institute Press, 2006).

[15] *Naval Technology*, 'Admiral Gorshkov Class Frigates', <https://www.naval-technology.com/projects/admiral-gorshkov/>, accessed 13 November 2021.

[16] Based on the ground-based version of the Monolit radar, the 3K41 is the sea version. See Michael Petersen, 'Russia's Naval Renewal', <https://mscconference.com/wp-content/uploads/MSC18-presentations/NATO-3-Petersen-Russian-Navy.pdf>, accessed 13 November 2021.

credible combatant in contemporary conflict.[17] While yet to enter service, the Project 23550 will add to the Northern Fleet's ASuW capabilities. Additionally, the containerisation of missiles, such as the Klub-K, raises the possibility of icebreakers being used as missile launchers.[18] However, the Northern Fleet's capacity for surface-to-surface engagement is still somewhat limited.

The Pacific Fleet has 15 corvettes of the *Grisha-* and *Tarantul-*classes. While limited in terms of their organic radar – capable of a reported 90–250 km detection range – the *Tarantuls* can serve as launchers for the Moskit cruise missile, as well as the KH-35, and can potentially add value to an ASuW effort if cued in by other assets.[19] The fleet also has three of Russia's newer *Streguschiy-*class corvettes, capable of launching the KH-35, as well as a *Sovremenny* and several *Udaloy* ASW destroyers.

In addition to the vessels discussed above, the Kalibr-equipped Project 23550 needs to be considered. At least two vessels are being built, along with those of the border protection force, which can provide peacetime tracking and sea control.

Nonetheless, given the limitations of Russia's surface forces, its force structure in the High North will be reliant on air, ground and subsurface assets. The authors have identified two locations on Alexandra Land and Kotelny where Russia has deployed the Bastion-P coastal defence system. These assets are likely under the aegis of the 536th Coastal Missile Brigade.[21] Though the authors were not able to establish a positive ID, it has been reported that Bal and Bastion coastal defence systems held under the 536th are also deployed on the Kola Peninsula and on Yuzhny Island, which is likely given their strategic importance.[22]

The most important component of Russia's maritime strike capability in the Arctic, however, is air-based assets. The 40th Mixed Aviation Regiment based at Olenya appears to control the majority of the joint command's Tu-22 M3 bombers. This would amount to a force of 30 bombers. The MIG-31K, which is a VKS asset, could also fall under the

---

[17] Paul Schwartz, *Russia's Contribution to China's Surface Warfare Capabilities: Feeding The Dragon* (Washington, DC: CSIS, 2015), pp. 15.

[18] Rosoborronexport, 'Club-K Container Missile', <http://roe.ru/esp/catalog/marina-de-guerra/armas-de-la-nave/klab-k/>, accessed 20 May 2021.

[19] Rossobornexport, '3TS-25E', <http://roe.ru/eng/catalog/naval-systems/shipborne-electronic-systems/3ts-25e/>, accessed 20 May 2021. Note that Rossobornexport may well publish overly optimistic estimates, meaning that real numbers may be even lower.

[20] The 9M-100 can be quad-packed. The exact mix of capabilities is unknown.

[21] Authors' OSINT analysis.

[22] Thomas Nilsen, 'Russia Deploys Missile System 70 km from Norway's Vardø Radar', *Barents Observer*, 7 August 2019.

Table 6: Anti-Surface Warfare Relevant Assets of the Northern Fleet

Class	Active	Radar (Not Including Fire Control)	Effective Detection Range Against Surface Vessels (Approx.)	Strike Capabilities	Defensive Missiles
Kirov	1(2)	MR-800, MR-710, MR-320	150-300 km	20 P-700 Granit	96 SA-N-6 48 SA-N-20 40 SA-N-4 60 SA-N-9
Gorshakov	2(2)	Monolit 3K41 OTH surface search 5P-20 K air-defence radar 5P-27 Passive Phased Array	250-450 km	16 Kalibr/ Oniks/Zircon	32 VLS cells capable of holding 9M96/9M-100[20]
Sovremenney	1(1)	MR-212 MR-750	150 km	8 SS-N-22 Sunburn	32 Uragan (SA-N-7) SAM launchers
Slava	1(1)	MR-600 Voskhod air/surface search radar, MR-710 Fregat-M air/ surface search radar	100 km	16 P-500 Bazalt	8 BS-300F launchers (4 ZIF-122 4K33 Osa-M SAM system launchers (40 9M33 missiles)
Udaloy I/II	2(4)	MR-750 MR-212	150 km	8 SS-N-22 Sunburn (*Udaloy II*)	SA-N-9 surface to air missiles

Source: Author generated

control of the 40th Mixed Aviation regiment but may also be fielded in the 98th Mixed Air Regiment.[23] Both the Tu-22 M3 and the MIG-31K are capable of launching the Kinzhal, an air-launched version of the Iskander quasi-ballistic missile, which can target surface vessels at 2,000 km ranges. The missile's quasi-ballistic trajectory, which exploits the seams between lower-tier air defences and upper-tier BMD interceptors, makes it a particularly difficult target for active defences to intercept and if accurately cued, the Kinzhal could have effects on the regional balance of power comparable to the DF-21D. But as of 2018, only 10 MIG-31 interceptors have been converted to MIG-31Ks capable of carrying the

---

[23] Alexey Ramm, 'Kak aviatsiya zashchishchayet rossiyskoye Zapolyar'ye' ['How Aviation Protects the Russian Arctic'], Wings of the Arctic, 18 June 2021, <https://nvo.ng.ru/armament/2021-02-18/5_1129_aviation.html>, accessed 29 November 2021.

Figure 11: Russian Warships at Severomrosk on 10 May 2021

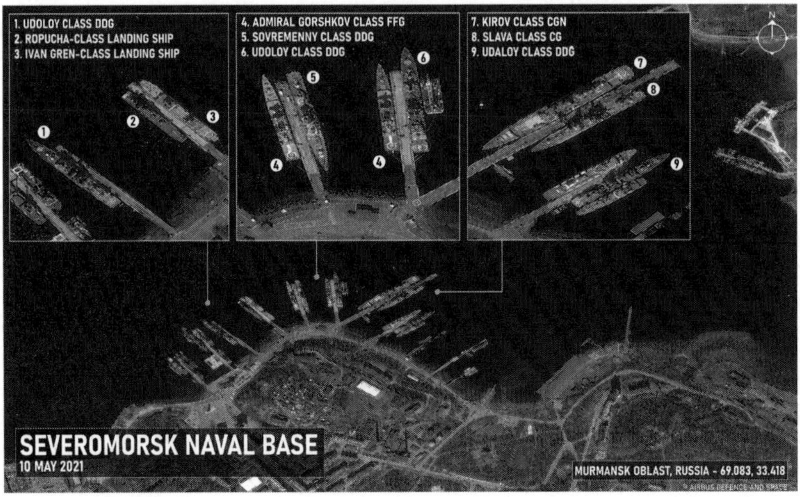

Source: Airbus Defence and Space and authors'

Kinzhal. This means that the bulk of the interceptors currently in the Arctic probably cannot deploy the Kinzhal.[24]

The Northern Fleet Joint Strategic Command also has operational control over the 279th and 100th Shipborne Fighter Regiments, based out of Severomorsk-3, where MIG-29Ks and SU-33s are respectively deployed. While primarily built to operate from Russia's aircraft carrier, the *Admiral Kuznetsov*, the SU-33 will in all probability have to operate from land bases given the chronic difficulties in maintaining the aircraft carrier.[25] The MIG-29, similarly, will probably operate from land bases rather than from the carrier for which it was built. Both aircraft can carry the KH-41 short-range supersonic ASCM on eight and 12 hardpoints, respectively, though in all likelihood they would have to get too close to a vessel in wartime to avoid interception before launch.[26] However, in peacetime, when involved in activities such as buzzing naval vessels, the threat posed by the ASCMs of the SU-33 could likely force foreign

---

[24] *TASS*, 'Ten MIG-31 Fighter Jets Fitted with Kinzhal Air-Launched Missile on Test Combat Duty', 5 May 2018.
[25] Ben Brimelow, 'Russia Is Desperately Trying to Save its Only Aircraft Carrier – That's Outdated and Plagued With Problems', *Business Insider*, 17 April 2018.
[26] Mark Episkopos, 'Why Russia's SU-33 Fighter Was a Failure', *National Interest*, 3 November 2020.

Figure 12A: The 40th Mixed Aviation Regiments Backfire Bombers at Olenya

Source: Airbus Defence and Space and authors'
Note: The number of bombers, 32, stayed constant across multiple images taken over a year, of which this one is a sample. This suggests that this sample is representative of the bases permanently assigned TU-22s.

Figure 12B: The 40th Mixed Aviation Regiments Backfire Bombers at Olenya

Source: Airbus Defence and Space and authors'

commanders to behave with caution along the NSR significantly.[27] The 98th Guards Separate Mixed Aviation Regiment and the 174th Guards Fighter Regiment based out of Monchegorsk field the SU-24 and MIG-31BM, respectively.

Although this will be more fully discussed in aviation-specific chapters, Russia also maintains a capacity for airlift in the High North through the 403rd Separate Mixed Aviation Regiment. This means that missile systems such as the Bastion-P can be moved at fairly short notice, given the availability of heavy-lift aircraft needed to move TELS.[28] Russia maintains a growing network of air bases in the Arctic. This means that it will likely be able to reallocate and disperse its air forces from a fairly narrow concentrated subset of the total number of bases in a crisis or wartime. In addition to complicating any attempts at suppression, this means that Russian bombers and fighters will operate relatively closely from friendly bases, ensuring longer loiter times and partially compensating for the relative lack of numbers.

In addition to torpedoes, the SSNs and SSGNs of Russia's Northern and Pacific Fleets can contribute to a long-range surface strike effort. SSGNs such as the *Yasen*, equipped with eight VLS silos, will be able to deploy the Kalibr, Oniks and Zircon cruise missiles. The SSGN can carry 32 Oniks or 40 Kalibrs or an unspecified number of Zircons when the missile enters service.[29] The *Oscar* was designed to carry 24 Granit ASCMs. Refits underway will see two Oscar II SSGNs capable of launching the P-800 join the fleet. While it is unclear how many P-800s the Oscar can carry, the likely introduction of the SM-315 triple-launcher would suggest about 72.[30] Boats such as the Improved Kilo can also launch four Kalibrs from their torpedo tubes.[31] The improved Akula will also have the ability to launch the Kalibr.

---

[27] In scenarios short of war, commanders cannot engage aircraft, meaning that they have to allow them to get in range and risk consequences if there is an escalation. This tends to take a psychological toll on operators, see Geoff Ziezulewicz, 'Russian Jet Buzzes US Warship in the Black Sea', *Navy Times*, 1 February 2021.

[28] Robert Dalsjö, Christopher Berglund and Michael Jonsson, *Bursting the Bubble: Russian A2/AD in the Baltic Sea Region: Capabilities, Countermeasures, and Implications* (Stockholm: FOI, 2018), p. 29.

[29] H I Sutton, 'Pr885 Severodvinsk Class', *Covert Shores*, 13 April 2019, <http://www.hisutton.com/Pr885_Severodvinsk_Class.html>, accessed 13 November 2021.

[30] H I Sutton, 'Oscar II SSGN', *Covert Shores*, 29 June 2019, <http://www.hisutton.com/OSCAR-II_SSGN.html>, accessed 13 November 2021.

[31] *Naval Recognition*, 'Kolpino Russian Submarine Trains Kalibr Anti-Ship Missile Fire', September 2020; Vavasseur, 'Russia's Akula-Class Submarines to Fire Kalibr Cruise Missile Following Upgrade'.

Figure 13: Russia's Network of Air- and Ground-Based Sea Denial Assets in the High North

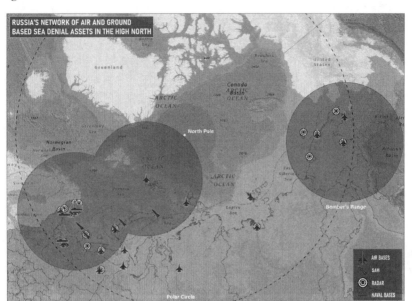

Source: Author generated
Note: Range radiuses are for bombers, with the assumption being that a single bomber operates for the whole of a given day without relief. The radiuses are shorter than the bombers' maximum range to account for loiter time.

Collectively, these assets can in principle build a layered barrier defence around the Arctic, and particularly in the west. The longest-ranged assets, the Kinzhal, can threaten large surface vessels at 2,000 km, potentially jeopardising surface operations in the Barents and Norwegian Seas from unassailable positions deep within the Arctic. Surface vessels, SSGN- and SSN-launched cruise missiles could, similarly, build an outer zone of sea denial around Scandinavia from positions within or slightly beyond the Arctic. Closer to Russia, ground-based missiles at Arctic chokepoints, as well as attacks by SSKs and fighter aircraft such as the SU-24 and SU-33, could further wear down hostile surface vessels.[32]

This system will only be effective, however, if accurate cueing and command and control (C2) is provided to the mix of assets discussed.

---

[32] The authors assume that SU-33s and SU-24s will be used against an already attritted force as, should this not be the case, they would suffer heavy attrition themselves given their short ranges.

Figure 14: The Growth of Kotelny's Temp Air Base Between 2014 and 2020

Source: Maxar Technologies and authors'

Russia's Reconnaissance Strike Complex

The system of sensors and C2 nodes on which Russia's ability to achieve maritime domain awareness depends will be critical to Russian efforts to control the High North during a crisis or wartime. It is arguably here that Russia is at its most limited. While the theoretical reach of Russia's strike capabilities could allow it to create effective control over large swathes of the Arctic and contest the adjoining seas, its ability to track moving targets at long ranges is somewhat limited. There are questions about the C2 structure and networking which enables the effective operation of the system architecture.

These problems become more acute the further away from Russia's shores a force moves. Close to Russian shores, ground-based systems such as the Monolit-B based on Yuzhny Island and Alexandra Land and surface-based radar can in all likelihood track targets out to 700 km from the Russian mainland.[33] Beyond this point, Russian forces would be dependent on surface air- and space-based surveillance to track surface vessels. Submarines could also identify surface targets but, given the potential for adversary SIGINT to locate them based on transmissions, the authors assume that they will be less likely to transmit information when at sea. In all likelihood, satellites will be a critical enabler for Russian long-range targeting beyond its bastions, much in the way that during the

---

[33] A Monolit-B on Yuzhny Island can track targets out to 450 km and if placed on Yuzhny – itself at some distance from the mainland – could track targets further out. A *Gorshkov* frigate or a *Sovremenny* equipped with an OTH system can track targets to a similar distance but can transit further from Russian shores to do so.

Soviet era the Legenda and RORSAT satellites were deemed crucial to the effective operation of SSGNs and other strike platforms. It is also worth mentioning that Russia's Polsodnyukh and Kontainer OTH radars can play some role in the early identification of surface targets – though the latter is not optimised for surface search and is primarily an air-defence asset. Nonetheless, OTH radar such as Australia's Jindalee have been used to track surface targets based on backscatter. While capable of operating at ranges of up to 3,000 km, OTH backscatter radar provides poor resolution due to factors such as surface clutter. Therefore, any returns from an OTH radar could have an error radius of up to 40 km. Nonetheless, these assets could be used to identify flight activity around vessels such as aircraft carriers and to cue in air- and space-based assets.[34]

Russia's primary satellite constellation, the Liana system, consists of the Pion and the Lotos S1 ELINT satellites. At present, only the smaller Lotos has actually been launched, with two currently active and a further four expected to enter service. Russian literature suggests that a Liana constellation should consist of at least two Lotos and two Liana satellites – suggesting that in principle the aspiration would be to build a matching number of Liana systems. Delays and overruns, however, make this an unlikely aim in the near term, with only one Liana satellite currently in progress.[35] Russia also fields two Kosmos optical satellites, both of which may have exceeded their operational length of service.[36] Russia's older Tselina and Legenda satellites could provide target locations with an accuracy of 30 km and a bearing error of up to 20 km.[37] While the resolutions of the Pion and Lotos satellites are highly classified, unverified Russian sources have claimed that the Liana constellation is vastly more accurate than the Soviet-era constellations, yielding accuracies of 1-3 m.[38] The authors deem this highly unlikely, but accept the likelihood of a significant improvement in capability. They have used the Chinese Yaogan constellation, launched during a similar time period with an error radius of 10 km, as a benchmark assumption. This is a crude assumption, but likely to be broadly representative.[39]

---

[34] Sidharth Kaushal, 'Persistent Engagement and Strategic Raiding: Leveraging the UK's Future Carrier Strike Capability to Effect', *RUSI Occasional Papers* (April 2020).
[35] Bart Hendrickx, 'The Status of Russia's Signals Intelligence Satellites', *Space Review*, 5 April 2021.
[36] Bart Hendrickx, 'Upgrading Russia's Fleet of Optical Reconnaissance Satellites', *Space Review*, 10 August 2020.
[37] V Bychkov and V Cherkashin, 'K voprosu o sisteme morskoy kosmicheskoy razvedki i tseleukazaniya' ['On the Issue of the Maritime Space Reconnaissance and Target Designation System'], *Nautical Collection* (Vol. 2, 2021), pp. 53-61.
[38] Hendrickx, 'The Status of Russia's Signal Intelligence Satellites'.
[39] S Chandrashekar and Soma Perumal, 'China's Constellation of Yaogan Satellites & the Anti-Ship Ballistic Missile: May 2016 Update', International Strategic and

Modelling of the revisit rates of five triple Chinese satellite constellations, which form part of the Yaogan system, suggests that the system can make 18 contacts with a vessel in the Western Pacific in a given day and cover 3,500 km at any given time.[40] It is reasonable to assume a significantly more limited Russian constellation will, even considering that the area they are surveying is marginally smaller than the Western Pacific, make a fraction of this number of contacts. Should Russia have three two-satellite clusters operational, this number will increase. However, the smaller numbers and lower altitudes of Russian satellites make it unlikely that they acquire targets at the same rate as their Chinese counterparts.[41] For all their limitations, Russia's ELINT satellites will provide at least intermittent coverage against surface assets at long ranges. Against vessels forced to operate within a bounded area – for example, frigates patrolling a chokepoint – the surveillance challenge may be easier. Russia's major limitations still appear to lie in obtaining granular data. Russia currently operates two Persona EO satellites, which are to be replaced with the Razdan in the 2020s.[42] The limitations of its constellation of EO imaging satellites, coupled with the fact that Russia has no plans to procure SAR satellites capable of all-weather functioning, and is currently reliant on a single Kondor SAR satellite for high-resolution imaging, will significantly limit Russia's ability to do more than identify vessels at long ranges using space-based assets alone.[43] Russia's civilian satellites could be leveraged as well – and some sources suggest they would be. However, civilian systems, including the Resurs-M, Meteor and Kanopus-K, have uncued revisit rates of two to three days.[44] That said, against vessels that have had their mobility artificially reduced – because they are on-station near a key barrier, for example – this limited constellation could potentially

---

Security Studies Programme, National Institute of Advanced Studies, May 2016, p. 13.

[40] *Ibid.*

[41] The Pion and Lotos can reach altitudes of 700–900 km. See *GolbalSecurity*, 'Lotos-S', <https://www.globalsecurity.org/space/world/russia/lotos-c.htm>, accessed 10 May 2021; on ELINT and SIGINT satellite sensor geometries, see A Andronov, 'American Geosynchronous SIGINT Satellites', translated by Allen Thompson, *Zarubezhnoye Voyennoye Obozreniye* [Foreign Military Review] (No. 12, 1993), <https://fas.org/spp/military/program/sigint/androart.htm>, accessed 13 November 2021.

[42] Hendrickx, 'Upgrading Russia's Fleet of Optical Reconnaissance Satellites'.

[43] The Kondor has a resolution of 6 m and a swath width of 20 km. See *SpaceFlight101*, 'Kondor Spacecraft Overview', <https://spaceflight101.com/spacecraft/kondor/>, accessed 13 November 2021.

[44] Roscocmos, 'The Russian Space Remote Sensing Systems' presentation, Brussels, 17–18 October 2018.

deliver actionable imagery with greater regularity in the absence of adversary counterspace efforts.

Russia will therefore need to rely heavily on airborne and surface assets if it is to effectively cue in long-range strike assets such as the Kinzhal at their optimal ranges. Soviet ASuW concepts during the Cold War placed an emphasis on the role of aircraft such as the TU-95MR with its MTsRS-1 Uspekh-1A X-band radar for maritime search.[45] While Russia operates 55 TU-95MR airframes, the authors could not identify the plane in the Arctic. However, one of the aviation regiments operating from Severomorsk-1 has the TU-95MR.[46] Although the aircraft operates primarily out of Engels Air Base (located near the Caucasus), it would likely play a role in any Russian effort at surface control within the Arctic. The onboard sensors of a platform such as the TU-22M3 or the IL-38N can also in principle detect targets at ranges of up to 200 nm – though this would place these assets within range of adversary aircraft and potentially shipboard defences. Surface vessels, particularly those equipped with OTH radar, can also provide tracking over ranges of several hundred kilometres, though the distances that these vessels venture out will likely be affected by factors such as their endurance and vulnerability to adversary airpower.

A second consideration is the speed with which Russia can aggregate the data it receives and pass it on to launch platforms. This can manifest itself in two ways. The first problem is the ability to quickly pass information to specific systems. Platforms such as SSGNs will have particular difficulties in this regard. The use of a floating wire antenna to receive transmissions exposes these assets to detection and data latency issues will increase the circular error probable of a target's location.[47] The second has more to do with Russia's progress towards a network-centric C4ISR system. While this end-state has received significant attention and resourcing since 2008 after being identified as a core priority by then-Defence Minister Anatoly Serdyukov, significant impediments to the fielding of a network-centric system of systems still bedevil Russia.

---

[45] Carlo Kopp, 'Tupolev TU-95 and TU-142 Bear', *Air Power Australia*, Technical Report APA-TR-2007-0706, April 2012, <http://www.ausairpower.net/APA-Bear. html#mozTocId258676>, accessed 13 November 2021.

[46] The unit had this asset during the Cold War. On current basing, see Russian Forces, 'Russian Strategic Nuclear Forces', <http://russianforces.org/aviation/>, accessed 9 April 2021. Although a blog is an unsatisfactory source, the contributors are members of the Russian academy and uniformed military, justifying its use in this case. Also, the authors conducted satellite imaging of at least one TU-95 at Severomorsk-1.

[47] Dennis Gormley, Andrew Erickson and Jingdong Yuan, 'A Low-Visibility Force Multiplier: Assessing China's Cruise Missile Ambitions', *Strategic Studies Quarterly* (Vol. 8, No. 2, Summer 2014), p. 52.

Russia's industrial base faces an impact from shortcomings in areas such as advanced micro-components.[48] Indeed, individual services have invested in tailored C2 systems – such as the air force's Andromeda-D – which are an impediment to multidomain integration between the VKS and naval assets which is critical to ensuring that land-, sea- and air-based assets can be coordinated.[49] Finally, the fact that some of the platforms executing a maritime denial approach are Soviet-era legacy systems acts as a further impediment to networking.[50]

At long ranges of over 1,500 km from Russian shores, where targeting an ASBM will require the effective cueing of space-based satellites, ground-based OTH radar and MPAs, the limitations of Russia's ability to track surface vessels will be at their most acute. However, particularly when search parameters are narrowed, Russian assets can be cued effectively, if intermittently. This is noteworthy given that it would only require marginal attrition of the already-limited frigate barriers at the GIUK Gap to open the way for more aggressive submarine operations. Closer to Russian shores, the challenge of targeting is simplified by two factors. The areas that Russian surveillance assets have to scan become smaller as a force moves into the narrower seas of the NSR and adjoining areas. It is nonetheless the authors' finding that the Russian A2/AD system still functions more as a cluster of partially integrated platforms that will limit its capacity for ASuW in the High North.

NATO

NATO's capacity for ASuW on Russia's northern flank is dependent on both time and geographical factors, as well as the Allies' overarching concept of operations. The Alliance's competitive position opposite Russia depends in part on how quickly it can mobilise ASuW capabilities. In terms of the parties' respective peacetime postures, Russia enjoys a substantial advantage over NATO in terms of available assets. This is because of its geographical position. In a high-intensity conflict, however, NATO can deploy a formidable suite of ASuW assets across domains, though much depends on the speed with which it mobilises them. Geography is a major factor also at higher levels of escalation, with Russia enjoying relative control over the central portions of the Arctic and more limited command over the western far eastern sectors. Finally, a NATO approach

---

[48] Roger McDermott, 'Tracing Russia's Path to a Network-Centric Military Capability', The Jamestown Foundation, 4 December 2020.
[49] *Ibid.*
[50] Roger McDermott, 'The Revolution in Russian Military Decision-Making', The Jamestown Foundation, 12 March 2021.

emphasising defensive sea control – containing Russia's Northern Fleet – sees the Alliance suffer significant losses in the early stages of a campaign. These will be sufficient to enable subsequent Russian activities such as submarine sorties beyond the Arctic. But a NATO approach that emphasises offensive sea control, by contrast, sees comparatively more limited Alliance losses and the effective elimination of Russia's surface forces. This could serve an enabling function for subsequent NATO air and subsurface operations in the region.

Although recent exercises conducted by member states in the region, and actions such as the reconstitution of the US Navy Second Fleet all point to the increased importance placed on the region by NATO, the Alliance still has a more limited potential for surface power projection in the region than Russia does.[51] In terms of a peacetime presence, NATO has approximately 22 civilian and coast guard icebreakers compared with Russia's 40.[52] This may change with recent steps by the US to reinvigorate its coast guard's icebreaking capability.[53] While not particularly relevant to high-intensity scenarios, icebreakers and ice-rated naval vessels could be critical to ensuring that surface assets can conduct activities such as freedom of navigation operations or presence missions in disputed territories. Given recent disagreements between Russia and certain NATO members over the former's attempts to impose rules governing the activity of commercial vessels through the NSR, this presence function may be important.[54]

In terms of warfighting assets, in the context of a military clash either inside or beyond the Arctic, NATO could probably mobilise up to 30 surface combatants in the early stages of a conflict in line with the demands of the Alliance's readiness initiative. This would include one or two carrier strike groups generated from the aircraft carriers held by the US, the UK and France, of which it is assumed at least one should be available all year round.[55] This force would be broadly comparable to the maritime

---

[51] On recent exercises, see Jim Garamone, 'US–British Arctic Exercise Shows US Concern for Region', *Department of Defense News*, 7 May 2020; on the Second Fleet, see *Maritime Executive*, 'US Reactivates 2nd Fleet to Counter Russian Navy', 31 December 2019.

[52] Paul C Avey, 'The Icebreaker Gap Doesn't Mean America Is Losing in the Arctic', *War on the Rocks*, 28 November 2019.

[53] *Navy Times*, 'Congress Oks New Icebreakers for the Coastguard', 15 December 2020, <https://www.navytimes.com/news/your-navy/2020/12/15/congress-oks-new-arctic-icebreakers-for-coast-guard/>, accessed 28 November 2021.

[54] Mark Lanteigne, 'The Changing Shape of Arctic Security', *NATO Review,* 28 June 2019.

[55] Hagstöm Frisell and Pallin (eds), *Western Military Capability in Northern Europe 2020*, p. 87; the UK CSG has effectively been committed to NATO, see UK Ministry

component of Exercise *Trident Juncture*, which operated under STRIKFORNATO and included 25 combatants, including a carrier strike group and an expeditionary strike group.[56] Over a longer period of several months the number of ASuW capable assets could expand substantially, with estimates of the force required to roll back a major Russian offensive in Europe typically ranging from 70–100 major combatants.[57] Not all these assets would necessarily be devoted to High North missions, with tasks such as patrolling the approaches to the Baltic Sea and the Mediterranean likely to draw on Allied resources. While it is difficult to know precisely how many surface assets would be devoted to the High North, because it is context dependent, the authors can describe the broad contours of such a force. Exercises such as *Formidable Shield* and *Trident Juncture* are instructive here. The exercises respectively coordinated the activities of up to 13 vessels in a simulated air and missile threat and 25 vessels in a joint operation to retake territory in the High North. As such, a notional force of 25–30 vessels, of which 13 are air-defence capable DDGs, might serve as a minimum number of air-defence capable vessels devoted to the northern theatre given the nature of the air and missile threat.[58]

Under the assumption that either the UK or France can generate a carrier strike group and commit it to tasks such as fleet air defence in the High North, this would entail the allocation of five warships to the region. For the purpose of this study, the authors also presume that the UK allocates its third available Type-45 DDG to the region.[59] The authors also presume that the French navy will allocate at least one air-defence destroyer to the region and that the US Navy – while initially constrained as discussed in previous chapters – will eventually allocate up to eight DDGs as a conflict progresses beyond its initial weeks.[60] The presence of a US CSG and an expeditionary strike group are also likely over a longer

---

of Defence, *CP411 Defence Command Paper: Defence in a Competitive Age* (London: The Stationery Office, p. 40).

[56] NATO, 'STRIKFORNATO Exercises Integration of Carrier Strike Group Eight', 2018, <https://sfn.nato.int/trje18-8>, accessed 13 November 2021.

[57] Hagstöm Frisell and Pallin (eds), *Western Military Capability in Northern Europe 2020*, p. 90; Barrie et al., 'Defending Europe: Scenario-Based Capability Requirements for NATO's European Members'.

[58] NATO, 'NATO Ships Start Missile Defence Drill Off Scotland', 8 May 2019.

[59] Assuming a 50% readiness level for the UK's six Type-45 DDGs.

[60] Based on the assumption that two of the four *Arleigh Burkes* at Rota are available and that a further two can be expedited to Europe. Over the course of a conflict, the authors assume that, at a readiness level of 50% and with the imperative to focus on Asia, the 90-ship fleet of DDG-51s and CG-47s can generate a further 15 vessels for European operations, which are evenly split between the Mediterranean, the Baltic and the High North.

time period. The time horizons for AsuW – and the presumed vessel allocation – are longer than those thought in Chapter II because it is reasonable to expect submarine breakouts to occur early in a conflict. Regional navies, such as Norway's and Denmark's, would likely contribute up to two surface combatants, though these would likely be allocated to ASW functions. The authors also work on the assumption that navies such as the German and Italian navies maintain a primary focus on regions such as the Baltics and the Eastern Mediterranean under all circumstances.

A major consideration is the fact that most NATO vessels will be outranged by Russian counterparts. Though this may change with the introduction of the Long Range Anti-Ship Missile (LRASM) aboard US vessels and with progress on the Anglo–French interim strike weapon, for the short to medium term, vessels equipped with older Harpoon ASCMs will find themselves outranged.

Airpower can partially compensate for this. Overall, the authors assume that NATO can deploy at short notice 21 combat air squadrons in the High North. NATO members have paid particular attention to equipping air-based assets with anti-ship capabilities, with the US Air Force practising launching the LRASM from its B1B.[61] Notably, the B1B is held under the USAF's global strike command, and its potential use in a High North conflict illustrates the role that non-European commands, including NORTHCOM and INDOPACOM, can potentially play alongside European commands. While this chapter primarily examines the balance between Russia and NATO in the Western Arctic and High North, the potential role of these assets is examined.

The introduction of the Naval Strike Missile on Norway's F-35 fleet, and the surface strike capability of the French Dassault Rafale, show how fourth- and fifth-generation airpower can potentially offset Russia's range advantage.[62] The US is also expected to be able to deploy at short notice up to six combat aircraft squadrons to the High North. Given the recent optimisation of US assets for surface combat within the first island chain, it is likely that these aircraft will add to NATO's surface strike capability. In addition, NATOs SSNs which, as discussed in Chapter II, are highly survivable given the limitations of Russian ASW, can contribute to efforts to suppress the surface threat. Equally, air cover will be critical to mitigating the renewed backfire threat.

---

[61] Stephen Losey, 'USAF B1-B Lancers Practiced Anti-Ship Missile Strikes in Black Sea,' *AirForceTimes*, 1 June 2020, accessed 21 December 2021.
[62] *Naval Technology*, 'The Naval Strike Missile', <https://www.naval-technology.com/projects/naval-strike-missile-nsm/>, accessed 15 May 2021.

However, two factors are noteworthy. First, the availability of airborne assets capable of surface strikes is somewhat limited, especially given the range of missions that will draw on newer aircraft – Norway currently has 15 of its planned 52 F-35s. Second, both airfields and aircraft carriers will be subject to suppression by precision strike assets early in a conflict. This will force operations from longer distances, which will be restricted by issues such as tanker availability. Russia's vessels at sea are defended by a dense – if poorly networked – maritime IADS. The primarily subsonic anti-ship capabilities at NATO's disposal will mean that large numbers of scarce munitions will be needed to secure kills. This does not mean that this is not achievable, but that it will not be easy despite NATO's advantages in the air.

Both NATO and Russia therefore appear to face significant limitations in their capacity to control the waters in the western portion of the High North. Russia's strike capabilities are limited by a still maturing reconnaissance strike complex, while NATO's ability to sustain regional power projection has atrophied. Further along the NSR, however, the more constrained oceans in the central and eastern parts, coupled with Russia's advantages in terms of the proximity of air and naval bases, should enable it to gain sea control in both peacetime and war. The next section delves into the process by which these deductions can be reached.

Modelling a Russian A2/AD Campaign in the High North

To examine the impact of a Russian anti-access campaign in the High North, the authors used a stochastic version of Wayne Hughes's Salvo Combat Model. This model, which has been used to effectively analyse clashes such as the Battle of the Coral Sea and Midway to good effect has a demonstrable predictive accuracy when tested against historical cases.[63] The value of this model is its ability to generate accurate outputs based on few variables. The model is based on weighted averages of the size of the salvo, defensive capacity, staying power of naval vessels and relative information advantage. The model treats an operation as a series of salvo exchanges – placing primary analytical weight on the balance of strike defensive and scouting capabilities. This scarcity of variables lends itself to simulation, with a manageable list of key factors that enable the analyst to vary scope conditions. The salvo exchange model is itself scenario neutral and focuses mainly on the relative offensive and defensive capabilities of the opposing forces. But the effects of initiative

---

[63] Michael J Armstrong and Michael B Powell, 'A Stochastic Salvo Model Analysis of the Battle of the Coral Sea', *Military Operations Research* (Vol. 10, No. 4, 2005), pp. 27–37.

can be incorporated into the model, which is described more fully in the technical appendices.

For the purpose of analysis, the authors have considered two scenarios consistent with a NATO ambition for defensive and offensive sea control and a defensive- and forward-leaning Russian posture. The first envisages a Russian effort to disrupt ASW operations in the High North to limit the freedom of action of NATO forces in the Norwegian Sea that wants defensive sea control. The second envisages a Russian effort to deny the waters near its bastions to a NATO force, including at least one CBG conducting offensive operations against its vessels and regional infrastructure. In the former case, Russia is expected to enjoy a relative information advantage because NATO assets have sacrificed a degree of tactical mobility to meet the needs of defensive sea control. In the latter case, though Russia has a more dense network of sensors nearer its bastions, the limited ranges of the organic sensors of systems such as the ground-based Bastion-P, the loss of sensor coverage as assets are destroyed, and the limited numbers of available patrol aircraft all work to restrict engagement opportunities.[64] Moreover, if NATO adopts a forward posture this is likely to involve SSNs and SSGNs contributing to the disruption of Russian C4ISR by, for example, sinking vessels which might act as spotters and conducting strikes against ground-based radar. Equally importantly, in scenarios where it adopts a forward posture NATO sets the tempo of activity and thus can launch the first salvo in a contest.

The results show a seven-day interval – the first week of a clash. The model is broken down into a series of intervals, each corresponding with the engagements over a single day, with the summarised results concerning a week of high-intensity combat. The number of engagements for Russia assume two to three low-resolution contacts with major formations in a given day, allowing commanders to task other ISR assets and assess the desired strike package. By contrast, NATO is assumed to have more accurate and persistent ISR and is limited by range, not data.

NATO's anti-air warfare (AAW) performance is varied. This takes into account the difficulty of intercepting Russian missiles that travel at supersonic speeds, though even the authors' lower-bound estimates may downplay the difficulty of intercepting newer weaponry. By contrast, although models for both assumptions were run and presented results, as was the case for NATO, Russian AAW performance can realistically be assumed to be high. This is based on the relative advantages Russia enjoys against an Alliance with limited ASuW strike options.

---

[64] Kaushal, 'Persistent Engagement and Strategic Raiding', pp. 20–30.

The results of the modelling are summarised below.[65]

While these exchanges would harm the Northern Fleet's surface forces, NATO would sustain significant costs when it adopts a reactive posture, losing almost one-third of its surface vessels under worst-case scenarios. This could be particularly significant if major assets, such as aircraft carriers, are targeted. This happens despite the fact that NATO enjoys numerical superiority and significant advantages in several areas. NATO vessels' air- and missile-defence systems are better networked than their Russian counterparts, although progress remains to be made in this area.[66] NATO's relative dominance in the air partially offsets Russia's advantage of having forces close. Russian sea denial depends on a range of tools, including strategic bombers and ground-based assets, which means that the losses of surface vessels would have a greater operational significance for NATO.

It is somewhat easier to model NATO losses than Russia's, because Russian attrition at sea is a function of, among other things, the amount of airpower allotted to ASuW missions as well as the high effectiveness of NATO SSNs. Based on available literature, the authors assume that ASuW is treated as a subset of offensive counter-air and receives about 25% of allocations alongside tasks such as SEAD and DCA.[67] We also assume that two of the USAF's six mission-capable B1B bombers are allotted to sea-control missions and that they operate from the continental US, because of the strike threat to air bases in theatre. The impact of SSNs on surface losses is – with the exception of their use as cruise missile launchers and their potential to impact the information environment – not considered in the salvo models used. This is a limiting factor for both sides, but particularly for NATO because its submarines may be its most potent ASuW tool. It is not unreasonable to presume therefore that Russian losses would be higher than estimated if NATO opts to use its submarines in a forward role, while NATO losses are artificially high as surface vessels capable of contributing to salvos would be sunk by SSNs. As Russia loses a majority of its surface vessels in any case, under this scenario the inclusion of losses inflicted by SSNs is likely only to reinforce the conclusions of the authors' modelling. The fact that NATO's estimated losses are higher than

---

[65] The standard deviations were 0.64 and 0.24 for NATO and Russian losses, respectively.

[66] On IAMD, see Sidharth Kaushal, Archer Macy and Alexandra Stickings, 'The Future of NATO's Air and Missile Defence', *RUSI Occasional Papers* (July 2021).

[67] NATO, 'Allied Joint Doctrine for Air and Space Operations', AJP-3.3, April 2016, paras 1–9. Notably, NATO doctrine could benefit from clarity on this issue, see *Ibid.*, p. 12.

Table 7: NATO and Russian Surface Vessel Losses

	AAW Performance High (SSPK 0.8)	AAW Performance Poor (SSPK 0.6)
Information advantage Russia	**NATO losses** 5 ships **Russian losses** 3 ships	**NATO losses** 8 vessels **Russian losses** 6 ships
Information advantage NATO	**NATO losses** 3 ships **Russian losses** 5 ships	**NATO losses** 5 ships **Russian losses** 7 ships

Source: Author generated
Note: Modelling NATO and Russian Exchanges in the Early Stages of a Conflict suggests crippling losses to the northern fleet- though the fleet can inflict meaningful attrition. (Details of the modelling in Appendix 1)

likely, however, may reinforce the viability of a forward posture though more granular analysis may be needed to affirm this.

On the other hand, if a large portion of the SSN fleet is allocated to barrier defence, their ASuW role may be more limited. These vessels would still raise the risks to Russian assets of sailing beyond the Barents Sea, but would not preclude vessels within the bastion from conducting strikes against any forward-deployed NATO weapons system.

Platforms such as the Norwegian F-35A, which is likely to be equipped with the Joint Strike Missile, and UK F-35Bs equipped with the SPEAR-3 and U.S F-35Cs will likely prove survivable against Russian air defences. However, the effectiveness of munitions that they fire will be limited by the dense short-range defences of Russian vessels.[68] This is not to say that Russian surface forces will not suffer attrition from both the air and the subsurface, however – merely that the level of attrition can be mitigated to a degree. By contrast, the speed of super and hypersonic Russian missiles limit shipboard air defences on NATO vessels. This means that the impact of shipboard IAMD on Russian salvos would be far more limited.

In a reactive posture, however, NATO appears to take early losses which, while not devastating, could severely disrupt an effort centred on defensive sea control. The loss of five vessels under circumstances where Russia has an information advantage will likely have an impact on operations in other domains, and particularly the subsurface. Under the second assumption, NATO loses fewer vessels and inflicts more casualties than when it adopts a purely reactive posture. This is despite the density of Russian defences in the region. Over time, as defenders get more scouting opportunities, NATO casualties may well rise to

---

[68] Nathan Gain, 'JSM Anti-Ship and Land-Attack Missile Successfully Tested from F-35A', *NavalNews*, 22 March 2021.

unacceptable levels. However, this does suggest that NATO is better served by being proactive, not reactive.

Analysis

The model above represents an idealisation in several ways. First, it examines a geographical section of what could potentially be a wider theatre of operations. In practice, a conflict between Moscow and NATO could eventually include US operations against Russia's far east – though the constrained geography of the Bering Strait limits both sides' options in this regard. Moreover, important synergies between domains – captured by concepts such as the US's Multi Domain Operations and Joint All Domain Command and Control – are relatively difficult to capture with such models.[69] However, the purpose of such models is to underscore certain key aspects of the balance of power: namely the significant costs that Russian A2/AD can inflict on a task force that is attempting defensive sea control and the relative advantages to NATO if it adopts a proactive, as opposed to a reactive, approach.

The balance of power between Russia and NATO in each of these three scenarios varies. In grey-zone sub-threshold contingencies, which are not the subject of formal modelling but will be assessed qualitatively, Russia's advantages in terms of military presence tend to be decisive. Russia's capacity for peacetime presence is largely unmatched by NATO's, especially in the Arctic's central regions. In a competition to demonstrate presence, the availability of a large civilian icebreaker fleet coupled with a growing military capability in this area will prove critical. The presence of Russian sea-denial assets along the NSR means that any standoff in the region following an effort to conduct a freedom of navigation operation would be under the aegis of Russian local escalation dominance. Short of any party initiating a full-scale clash over the NSR, Russia can dominate all likely scenarios, including limited skirmishes.

In a high-intensity conflict scenario, circumstances appear to be more ambiguous. While the limitations of Russia's long-range reconnaissance strike complex would seem to suggest that vessels would become more vulnerable the closer they are to Russia, the modelling painted a more mixed picture. Vessels stationed within a given geographical area took heavier losses than those being offensive. This may partially reflect the fact that attackers can select the time and place for an engagement. Over

---

[69] US Naval Institute, 'Report to Congress on Joint All Domain Command and Control', USNI, 17 August 2021, <https://news.usni.org/2021/08/17/report-to-congress-on-joint-all-domain-command-and-control-3>, accessed 28 November 2021.

time, the risks of forward offensive action may equal or exceed those faced by vessels on picket duty. However, at least during raiding, the models suggest that offensive action delivers better results for NATO than passive sea control.

The elimination of vessels such as the *Kirovs* and *Goshkovs* could limit the precision strike threat to NATO territory, given the roles of these vessels as cruise missile launchers as well as a component of the Russian IADS. The loss of surface vessels could also force Russian planners to pull SSGNs back for ASuW operations to defend their bastions, which limits offensive options. The elimination of a component of Russia's AAW and ASuW capabilities could enable subsequent air and surface operations against the Russian High North at lower costs. However, the ground-based A2/AD system, as well as the threat posed by Russian strategic bombers, limits the freedom of action of NATO surface vessels even if the Northern Fleet suffers heavy attrition.

By contrast, however, under conditions where NATO attempts a more reactive approach, Russian assets inflict steady attrition on the force. While not impenetrable, the Russian anti-access system appears capable of inflicting sufficient attrition to limit the effectiveness of superior maritime forces. That said, its ability to prevent maritime forces from operating freely near Russian bastions does not preclude NATO from achieving significant effects with a pulsed raiding posture.

CHAPTER IV: THE BALANCE OF POWER IN THE AIR

Key Points

- Though heavily outmatched in the air, Russia enjoys some asymetrical advantages.
- Its ground- and sea-based IADS in the Western Arctic, operating in tandem with interceptors like the MIG-31BM, can force NATO tankers to operate at longer distances, limiting sortie rates.
- Russian precision strike capabilities can render operation from bases in Norway highly risky, meaning that NATO airpower will need to operate from further afield, or from the sea.
- As a result, Russia enjoys a favourable balance of power in the air over the western portions of the Arctic and the High North.
- In the Central and Eastern Arctic, Russian defences are much thinner, exposing Russia to the risk of this gap being exploited by bombers and submarine-launched cruise missiles.
- Russia may well be incentivised to suppress air bases in Greenland and Alaska pre-emptively using sea-launched cruise missiles to mitigate this risk.
- Like the other balances described, mutual vulnerability makes the air environment an offence-dominated one.

A key component of Russia's reinvigoration of its Arctic posture has been the construction of a network of air bases along Russia's Arctic periphery. Russia has, over the last decade, refurbished 13 air bases in the region, and has constructed what effectively amount to new facilities in areas such as Kotelny.[1] The Russian air force (VKS) and naval aviation deploy a range of airborne assets in the region, which will prove critical to surface control in the adjoining seas.

---

[1] Matthew Melino and Heather Connely, 'The Ice Curtain: Russia's Arctic Military Presence', CSIS, <https://www.csis.org/features/ice-curtain-russias-arctic-military-presence>, accessed 21 April 2021.

Moreover, Russia has also placed strategic SAM systems such as the S-400 in the region. The authors identified S-300 and S-400 regiments near Rogachevo, Kotelny and Tiksi Air Bases. In addition, the Northern Fleet holds three AA regiments at Severomorsk and Olenya, equipped with the S-300, S-400 and Pantsir systems. It has also been reported that the S-400 has been emplaced on Wrangel Island during exercises.[2] While the authors could not verify this, they were able to locate a Sopka radar on the island, and regard the co-location and presumable integration of a SAM system with an air-defence radar in a crisis scenario to be likely. Senior figures such as Admiral Alexander Moiseyev have asserted an eventual desire to create a protective SAM shield across the entirety of the Arctic.[3]

While operating with more capable aircraft, NATO will be disadvantaged in terms of geography and available infrastructure near the region. However, there are also significant gaps in Russia's own system of aircraft, surface-to-air systems and early-warning radar within the region which are particularly acute in the Central Arctic and make the region vulnerable to long-range bombers and submarine-launched strike assets.

Russian Capabilities and Infrastructure in the High North

Russia's Northern Fleet Joint Strategic Command and its Far Eastern Military Command field a significant capability suite for the conduct of defensive counter-air missions over the Western portions of the Russian Arctic. The construction of air bases within the region will allow assets to be surged, augmenting an IADS system that is already highly robust in areas such as the Kola Peninsula, though not, notably, across the expanse of the Arctic. However, the Russian air force and naval aviation have fallen behind both Western and, increasingly, Chinese competitors in areas such as the quality of air-to-air interceptors, airborne AESA radar and stealth capabilities. It is likely that, beyond the reach of a friendly IADS, Russian air forces will be increasingly uncompetitive against peer competitors.[4]

---

[2] Matthew Melino, Heather A Conley and Joseph S Bermudez Jr, 'Ice Curtain S-400 Deployments and Enhanced Defence of Russia's Western Arctic', CSIS, 30 March 2020, <https://www.csis.org/analysis/ice-curtain-s-400-deployments-and-enhanced-defense-russias-western-arctic-rogachevo-air>, accessed 28 November 2020.
[3] Malte Humpert, 'Russia Activates Newest S-300 Air Defence System in Arctic', *High North News,* 7 April 2020, <https://www.highnorthnews.com/en/russia-activates-newest-s-300-air-defense-unit-arctic>, accessed 10 March 2021.
[4] Justin Bronk, 'Modern Russian and Chinese Combat Air Trends', *RUSI Occasional Papers* (October 2020), pp. 20–35.

However, Russia's difficulties in generating assets capable of effective air-to-air engagement may be of somewhat less salience within the Arctic. That is because the Russian Arctic force structure appears to be set up less to conduct air-to-air engagements than to defend against long-range precision strike campaigns in tandem with a ground-based IADS and to contribute to a Russian strike campaign. The Northern Fleet Joint Strategic Command has been allocated flanker aircraft such as the SU-30 and SU-33, both held by the 279th Separate Shipborne Fighter Aviation Smolensk Red Banner Regiment, as well as two squadrons of MIG-29 K aircraft under the 100th Independent Shipborne Fighter Regiment, but Russia's aerial assets in the region – excluding bombers, transport and patrol aircraft – are primarily comprised of the MIG-31BM interceptor, which is optimised to operate within a Russian IADS to provide wide area defence against low-flying cruise missiles.[5] This is consistent with the wider Russian emphasis on deflecting conventional precision strikes on its northern flank.[6]

Under the current Russian command structure, defence of the Arctic will likely be conducted on a sectored basis by the Northern Fleet Joint Strategic Command and the forces held by the Pacific Fleet within the Far Eastern Military district. The 45th Air and Air Defence Forces Army, headquartered in Murmansk, is the organisation primarily responsible for air defence along much of the Arctic, while the Pacific Fleet will be responsible for the eastern parts.

The authors were able to use a combination of open-source methods – described in the Methodology section – to provide a broad overview of the assets which can be identified within the region. The fixed-wing air superiority, interceptor and unmanned reconnaissance assets fielded by the Russian VKS and naval aviation in and near the Arctic are summarised below.

A number of characteristics of this force are noteworthy. First, it is of note that Russia's Arctic oriented commands do not field its newest air-superiority aircraft such as the SU-35, and have a fairly limited number of SU-33 and MIG-29Ks at their disposal.[7] Of course, assets held in other military districts can be reallocated in wartime and, as discussed below, Russia's expansion and renovation of its Arctic infrastructure could

---

[5] For more information on the MIG-31BM, see *ibid.*; Russian assets identified by imaging, samples of which are provided in Figures 15A and 15B and cross-referenced with David Batashvilli, 'Russian Military Forces: An Interactive Map', Rondelli Foundation, <https://www.gfsis.org/maps/russian-military-forces>, accessed 9 May 2021.
[6] Michael Koffman, presentation given at RUSI Seapower Conference 2021, 25 February 2021.
[7] Authors' IMINT analysis.

Figure 15A: Aircraft of the 100th Regiment, 279th Regiment and 98th Air Regiment at Monchegorsk on 19 March 2021

Source: Maxar Technologies and authors'

Figure 15B: Aircraft of the 100th Regiment, 279th Regiment and 98th Air Regiment at Severomrosk-1 on 22 August 2020

Source: Maxar Technologies and authors'

Table 8: Major Russian Air Units in the Arctic

Unit	Location	Aircraft	Number (Approx.)
279th Shipborne Fighter Regiment	Severomorsk-3	SU-33	24 SU-33
100th Shipborne Fighter Regiment (subordinate to 279th)	Severomorsk-3	MIG-29K	24 MIG-29K
UAV Regiment	Severomorsk-3	Forpost, Orlan	n/a
New Regiment (planned)	Monchegorsk	MIG-31BM (potential)	MIG 31BM/K
98th Mixed Air Regiment	Monchegorsk	MIG-31BM SU-24M/MR SU-24MR	12 MIG-31BM 12 SU-24 SU-24MR

Source: Author Generated, Based on open source data and Satellite Imaging of Russian Facilities

certainly allow the accommodation of platforms rapidly surged from other regions. Nonetheless, the relative paucity of organic air superiority assets, when contrasted with the fact that Arctic-facing commands appear to hold a significant number of Russia's MIG-31BM, appears in part to reflect an operational judgement – namely that given the distances involved, the primary threat to the Russian Arctic is not aircraft per se but cruise missiles and other low observable long-range strike assets.[8]

This is notable given that, at least in principle, parts of the Russian Arctic could certainly be menaced by fixed-wing aircraft operating from bases in Scandinavia or, for that matter Alaska. One potential reason that fixed-wing operations from bases in these regions appear not to have received as much attention is that Russian planners might envision being able to suppress air operations in these adjacent regions through the aggressive and early use of strike capabilities.[9] This could be of particular utility with respect to limiting air operations from areas such as Norway and could, at a minimum, force NATO to operate from bases further out.[10] Operating at reach would, in turn, entail a heavy reliance on large tanker aircraft which cannot be dispersed or hidden in hardened air shelters like fighters can and are thus much more vulnerable to

---

[8] Authors' IMINT analysis.

[9] On Russia's approach to offensive counter air, see Dima Adamsky, *Moscow's Aerospace Theory of Victory: Western Assumptions and Russian Reality* (Washington, DC: CAN, 2021).

[10] Johan Norberg and Martin Goliath, 'The Fighting Power of Russia's Armed Forces', in Westerlund and Oxenstierna (eds), *Russian Military Capability in a Ten Year Perspective-2019*, p. 67.

Table 9: Russian Air Defence Units in the Arctic

Unit	Location	SAM Systems
1528th Anti-Aircraft Missile Regiment	Severodvinsk	S-400
583rd Anti-Aircraft Missile Regiment	Olengorsk	S-300 PM, S-300 PS
33rd Anti-Aircraft Missile Regiment	Rogachevo	S-400
Tiksi unit (unverified by authors)	Tiksi	S-300
99th Arctic Tactical Group	Temp	Pantsir

Source: Author generated, based on open source data and satellite imaging of Russian facilities

destruction on the ground. Tanker aircraft are also, depending on the location of their orbits, vulnerable to being shot down by strategic SAM systems.

A second plausible reason for the emphasis on long-range strike could be a growing confidence in Russia's network of ground-based air-defence systems in the region. While Russia's network of surface-to-air-missiles and radar will be discussed in greater depth, it is worth noting that the air defences of the Arctic have seen significant investment with S-300 PM and S-400 regiments being set up under the command of the First Air Defence Division at Severomorsk and an S-400 regiment stood up at Rogachevo and an S-300 regiment near Tiksi joining the force under the control of the 3rd Air Defence Division. The following sections discuss Russia's IADS in the Arctic and its capacity for offensive strike missions against air bases in the High North in greater depth.

The Russian IADS in the Arctic

Russia fields an increasingly robust ground-based air-defence network within the Arctic. At the core of this network are long-range strategic SAMs such as the S-300 and S-400. In addition, Russia also fields shorter-ranged defensive systems such as the Pantsir, which can provide shorter-ranged point defences around key targets. The inventory of SAMs organic to the OSK Server is as follows.

Russia's strategic SAM systems are often collocated with UHF radar, such as the Resonance-N, which can provide them with early warning at ranges in excess of their own organic radar. While the precise specifications of the Resonance-N are unknown, its manufacturers claim that it can provide early warning against a range of targets from stealth aircraft to hypersonic glide vehicles and cruise missiles. This is not entirely implausible and reflects Western experience in operating UHF radar at sites such as RAF Fylingdales. Against low observable targets like low-flying cruise missiles and low observable aircraft, the manufacturers

Figure 16: Disposition of Russia's IADS in the Arctic

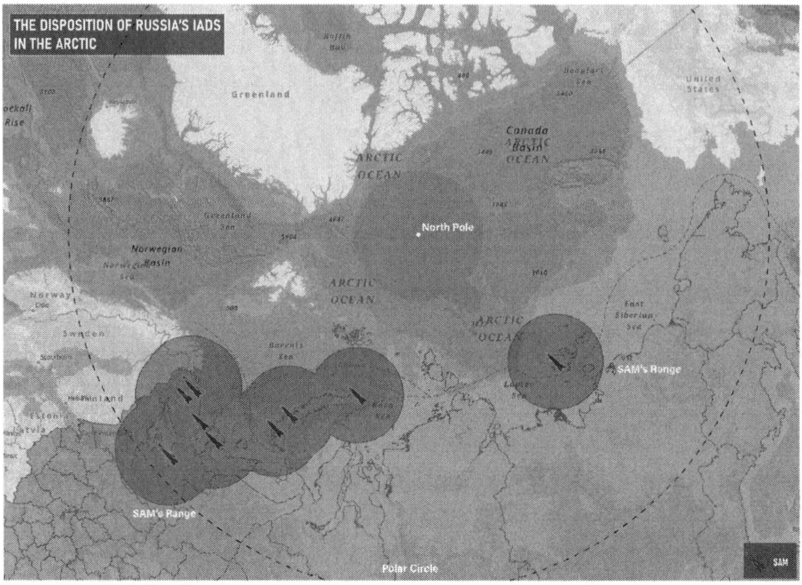

Source: Author generated, based on open source data and imaging of Russian facilities

posit a detection range of 100 km.[11] The authors have no way of verifying this claim, but deem it plausible in light of the fact that it is consistent with the modelling assumptions that have been employed in previous literature.[12] In the last several years, the 350-km range S-band Sopka-2 radar has also been emplaced on Kotelny and Wrangel Island. The radar primarily serves air traffic control roles but can also play an early-warning and intelligence-gathering function. This has the effect of plugging a gap that had existed in Russia's current early-warning posture.

In conjunction with larger early-warning Voronezh radar emplaced deeper within Russia, these assets can significantly improve warning times for air defenders.[13] While they lack the granularity to enable launch

---

[11] Rossoboronexport, 'Long Range Air Surveillance Radar "Resonance-NE" for Ballistic Missile Early Warning Systems and Low Observable Target Detection', <http://nic-rezonans.ru/wp-content/uploads/2020/10/eng-rls-resonance-n.pdf>, accessed 21 December 2021.
[12] See, for example, Michael Pelosi and Amy Honeycutt, 'Cruise Missile Integrated Air Defense System Penetration: Modelling the S-400 System', *International Journal of Aeronautics and Aerospace* (Vol. 4, 2017), pp. 1–20.
[13] The Voronezh series has wavelengths in the decimetre and metre band – enabling very long-range early-warning, albeit with low granularity. See, for example, Globalsecurity, 'Voronezh High Depot Readiness (HDR) Variants',

Figure 17: S-400 Battalion at Rogachevo

Source: Maxar Technologies and authors'
Note: In the interest of brevity, all imagery used to identify SAM and radar locations are not displayed; samples are used throughout the chapter.

decisions, they can significantly speed up air defenders' response cycles. As will be discussed later, while this does not necessarily impact the attrition inflicted on newer NATO aircraft, it significantly improves Russia's capacity for defence against long-range strike assets.

The second major source of offboard data for SAM systems in the region is likely to be the MIG-31BM. The Zaslon-M passive electronically scanned radar aboard the aircraft is optimised to detect low observable objects such as cruise missiles. Against targets with a 20m RCS – such as a tanker or AWACS – the radar has a detection range of 400 km, while its detection range against targets with an RCS of less than 0.5m – the average cruise missile, for example – is 60 km. Given that it can fly beyond Russian shores, unlike ground-based systems, this expands the effective coverage of Russia's sensor network substantially.[14] With 300 km range R-37 (AA-9 Amos) air-to-air missiles the MIG-31 can also

---

<https://www.globalsecurity.org/wmd/world/russia/voronezh-variants.htm>, accessed 21 December 2021.
[14] For more on the Zaslon, see Shepard Media, *The Concise Industry Guide to Radar Systems* (Derbyshire: Shepard Media, 2018), p. 14.

Figure 18: Sopka-2 Site on Kotelny

Source: Maxar Technologies and authors'

place large support aircraft such as AWACS and tankers at risk at long distances of 400 km – a characteristic it shares with ground-based SAMs.[15]

Effectively, the presence of these assets in Russia's Arctic force structure ensures that Russian air defenders should receive early warning of an air attack at distances of 3,000 km, and increasingly granular early-warning data from the triangulation of information from the Voronezh and shorter-range Sopka and Resonance-N radar at distances of 350–400 km from its shores.

Behind this early-warning layer, a forward deployed layer of assets, including the airborne MIG-31BM, but also Russia's surface fleet, can play a role in augmenting air defences. It is of course unclear to what extent air, sea and ground assets are networked within Russia. While the creation of a seamless cross-service tactical network was a key goal of the Serdukov reforms, this may face significant impediments in practice.[16] For example, the fact that the individual services have pursued different C4ISR networks may well pose an impediment to integration. However, it

---

[15] Globalsecurity, 'AA-9 Amos', <https://www.globalsecurity.org/military/world/russia/aa-9.htm>, accessed 21 December 2021.

[16] Roger McDermott, *Russian Perspectives on Network Centric Warfare: The Key Aim of Serdukovs Reforms* (Fort Leavenworth, KS: FMSO Books, 2011).

Figure 19: Russia's Early-Warning Radar Network in the High North

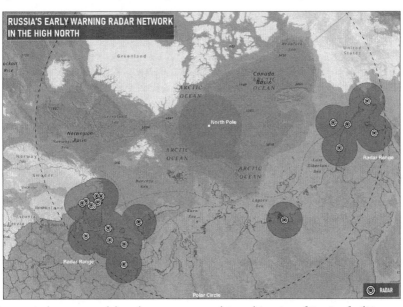

Source: Author generated, based on open source data and imaging of Russian facilities

is likely that assets such as the MIG-31BM can share data with ground-based SAM systems.[17] Moreover, even if they are not networked with other assets, Russia's maritime forces can provide an independently operating IADS at sea to augment their work.

The Northern Fleet's larger vessels, such as the *Kirov*, carry a maritime variant of the S-300 system equipped with 96 5V55RM SAMs, with semi-active radar homing and a range of up to 90 km.[18] The *Kirov* also carries 96 S-300 F and S-300FM launchers, which contain the 48N6 and 48N6E2 SAMs, capable of operating at a maximum range of 150 km. The platform also carries 64 3K95 short-range interceptors.[19] The S-300F is also present aboard the fleet's *Slava*-class cruiser, the *Marshal Ustinov*, which has 64 launchers capable of holding the 48N6, as well as the Osa

---

[17] Bronk, 'Russian and Chinese Combat Air Trends', p. 13.

[18] Navy Recognition, 'Russia's Kirov Class Cruiser *Admiral Nakhimov* to Be Fitted with 48N6DMK Missiles from S-400', <https://www.navyrecognition.com/index. php/news/defence-news/year-2015-news/november-2015-navy-naval-forces-defense-industry-technology-maritime-security-global-news/3232-russias-kirov-class-cruiser-admiral-nakhimov-to-be-fitted-with-48n6dmk-missiles-from-s-400. html>, accessed 21 December 2021.

[19] *Ibid.*

short-range point defence system fitted with the 30 km range 9M33M.[20] The range of these SAMs, coupled with the ability of the *Kirov* and *Slava* to launch them from forward positions, could allow significant portions of airspace over Norway and the Barents Sea to be denied to large aircraft like tankers and AWACS. The fleet's *Sovremenny* and *Udaloy* destroyers also contribute to its air-defence capability, albeit to a lesser degree. The *Sovremenny* is equipped with 48 Shtl missiles, which have a range of 48 km.[21] The *Udaloy* carries 64 VLS tubes for shorter-ranged 3K95 SAMs. These systems are more useful for the area defence of a formation at sea.

The Northern Fleet's newer surface vessels such as its *Gorshkov*-class frigates are equipped with a highly credible air-defence suite. The *Gorshkov*-class can launch the 120-km 9M96E missile used by the S-400 from its Redut VLS cells, along with shorter-range missiles such as the 9M96E and 9M100. This, coupled with the vessel's credible sensor suite, which includes the Poliment Active Phased Array Radar, can allow the *Gorshkov* to both protect smaller vessels and act as part of a forward layer of the Russian air-defence network.[22] The smaller vessels of the fleet, its *Grisha*-class corvettes, can launch 20 9M33M short-range interceptors.

The Pacific Fleet's larger vessels like the *Sovremenny*- and *Udaloy*-class DDGs have limited SAM capabilities. The fleet has, however, been the primary recipient of the new Steregusichiy Corvette which is equipped with 16 Redut VLS cells capable of launching the same missiles as the *Gorshakov*.[23] The organic radar of these vessels is, however, likely to be more limited given their size, suggesting, in the authors' estimation, the likely emplacement of the 9M100 on these vessels.

Behind this forward layer is Russia's ground-based network of surface-to-air missiles. The most formidable component of this network is based on the Kola Peninsula. The air-defence assets held at Severomorsk and Severodvinsk, comprised of the S-400 and S-300PMU, could in principle erect an anti-access barrier at ranges of up to 400 km against high-flying objects. While this might not impact fighter aircraft, it would

---

[20] Naval Technology, 'Slava Class Guided Missile Cruiser', <https://www.naval-technology.com/projects/slavaclassguidedmiss/>, accessed 12 April 2021.
[21] Naval Technology, 'The Sovremenney Class Destroyer', <https://www.naval-technology.com/projects/slavaclassguidedmiss/>, accessed 12 April 2021.
[22] *Naval News*, 'Admiral Gorshkov Frigate Qualifies Poliment-Redut SAM Against Air & Surface Targets', October 2018, <https://www.navyrecognition.com/index.php/news/defence-news/2018/october-2018-navy-naval-defense-news/6579-admiral-gorshkov-frigate-qualifies-poliment-redut-sam-against-air-surface-targets.html>, accessed 21 December 2021.
[23] Russian Ships Info, 'Project 20380', <http://russianships.info/eng/warships/project_20380.htm#>, accessed 12 April 2021.

Figure 20: 1528th AD Regiment SAM Site Severodvinsk

Source: Maxar Technologies and authors'

potentially impact targets such as AWACS and tankers – and have a knock-on effect on fighter operations.[24] Systems like the S-400, which operate digital rather than analogue radar, are significantly less vulnerable to jamming than older predecessors. An S-400 battalion possesses an S-band 91N6 Big Bird radar for target detection and acquisition at ranges of up to 600 km.[25] The battalion also possesses 1-2 92N6E fire control radars and a battalion level. The 92N6E can perform track while scanning operations and can track up to 100 targets in scan mode. It can provide precision tracking for six engagements concurrently. An S-400 regiment will typically contain eight launchers across two battalions, capable of launching both long-range SAMs such as the 400-km range 40N6 and as well as the shorter-range 9M96E and 9M96E2. Four 9M96E2 fit into a single launch canister, meaning that a given S-400 TEL can field between four and 16 missiles.[26] The precise loadouts of individual systems tend to vary.

---

[24] For a more detailed discussion see Chapter II.
[25] Radartutorial.eu, '91N6', <https://www.radartutorial.eu/19.kartei/06.missile/karte013.en.html>, accessed 21 December 2021.
[26] Missile Defence Advocacy Alliance, 'S-400 Triumf Air Defence System', <https://missiledefenseadvocacy.org/missile-threat-and-proliferation/todays-missile-threat/russia/russia-anti-access-area-denial/s-400-triumf-air-defense-system/>, accessed 21 December 2021.

Table 10: Total Active Fighter/Attack Aircraft Inventories by Generation in 2020

Country	3rd Gen	4th Gen	4.5th Gen	5th Gen	Total
Turkey	73	260	0	0	333
France	0	130	142	0	272
Italy	16	139	86	7	248
Greece	20	198	0	0	218
Germany	0	88	123	0	211
United Kingdom	0	46	139	13	198
Spain	32	0	146	0	178
Poland	0	99	0	0	99
Canada	0	0	77	0	77
Norway	0	57	0	10	67
Netherlands	0	61	0	2	63
Belgium	0	59	0	0	59
Other NATO Allies	0	132	28	0	196
Non-US NATO (Total)	**141**	**1,269**	**741**	**32**	**2,219**
USAF	0	887	0	281	1,168
USN	0	14	700	22	736
USMC	130	0	251	56	437
United States (Total)	**130**	**901**	**951**	**359**	**2341**
Total	**271**	**2,170**	**1,692**	**391**	**4,560**

Source: Daryl Press, 'The Evolving Air Balance in Europe'. presentation at RUSI Space and Missile Defence Conference 2020, London, 27 February 2020
Note: Aircraft numbers may have changed slightly since 2020. The table is meant to be illustrative of the aggregate balance.

The S-300, S-300 PM and S-300 PS systems at Severomorsk, Tiksi and Olengorsk are older. The S-300 PS is the oldest of the three. It is cued by the 5N63S Flap Lid B radar, which covers a 90-degree sector in a manner roughly analogous to the AN-SPY1.[27] A battery consists of a flap lid engagement radar as well as one 5P85S and two 5P85D TELs-with the latter slaved to the former. The system launches the 5V55 SAM. The S-300 PM saw the inclusion of the 5N64S Big Bird 3D search and acquisition radar. The system also includes the 5P85T TEL, which is a road mobile system built to be more rapidly set up and moved than earlier variants, enabling shoot and scoot tactics. A typical S-300 PM regiment contains three batteries – each equipped with up to 12 launchers carrying the 48N6 – along with a shared 5N64S, three battery level 76N6 low-level early-warning radars and 30N6E continuous wave pulse Doppler target acquisition fire control and engagement radars.[28]

---

[27] Carlo Kopp, 'Almaz S-300P/PT/PS/PMU/PMU1/PMU2 Almaz-Antey S-400 Triumf SA-10/20/21 Grumble/Gargoyle', Air Power Australia, <http://www.ausairpower.net/APA-Grumble-Gargoyle.html#mozTocId106894>, accessed 21 December 2021.
[28] FAS, 'S-300PMU', <https://fas.org/nuke/guide/russia/airdef/s-300pmu.htm>, accessed 21 December 2021.

Point defences such as the SA-22 Pantsir have also been identified by the authors as being part of the 1528th regiment and the 33rd Arctic tactical group. Given the large number of Pantsirs in service, this is likely a very small subset of the total. Russian air defences tend to use multistatic detection triangulating from a number of radars in order to counter low observability. Moreover, the effective networking of systems can create a whole that is greater than the sum of its parts by, for example, allowing a system such as the S-400 to 'launch on remote' based on a track from a forward deployed S-300 battery or a MIG-31BM.[29]

NATO Capabilities

NATO can field significant air forces that qualitatively outmatch their Russian counterparts and may well prove sufficient for certain tasks – for example, jeopardising the movement of Russian surface vessels beyond their bastions. However, as analysis in this section will illustrate, significant impediments to projecting power within the Arctic exist.

Analysis by other institutes has produced the estimate that NATO can generate 31–35 combat air squadrons at short notice. Over time, an increasing number of these squadrons will be comprised of fifth-generation assets. NATO air forces retain a significant capacity for air-to-air combat. They also exceed their Russian counterparts in terms of factors such as training. A rough lethality and vulnerability score for each type of aircraft in NATO's inventory is included below.

The composition of the air forces that NATO can generate to support operations in the High North, as well as the size of the force, is somewhat context dependent. NATO members such as Germany, France and the UK operate a substantial number of fourth-generation aircraft such as the Eurofighter Typhoon and the Rafaele. Norway and the UK operate the F-35, but the total non-US fifth-generation fighter fleet remains limited.

NATO's air and missile defences in the western portions of the High North include six Norwegian NASAMs batteries, as well as the IAMD capabilities of the NATO vessels which can deploy to the region. Vessels such as the Type 45, the *Arleigh Burke* and the FREMM Frigate all have area air-defence capabilities. They are equipped with the SAMP/T and Aegis systems respectively.

---

[29] Bronk, 'Russian and Chinese IADS', p. 10.

Analysing the Balance of Power in the Air

Although NATO maintains significant qualitative advantages over Russia in the air, Russia maintains geographical advantages in the western part of the theatre. Its vulnerability in the rest of the High North, and its reliance on limited numbers of MIG-31 interceptors could, however, open gaps in this part of the system – particularly if MIG-31s are destroyed on the ground by strikes from forward positioned SSNs and SSGNs, for example. In the Western Arctic, should a conflict either erupt in or spread to the High North, NATO aircraft conducting SEAD missions would need to rely on relatively vulnerable air bases in Norway in order to conduct missions. These bases would fall within the range of a panoply of long-range strike assets including the Kalibr and KH-101, and their air defences could only hold this threat at bay for a limited period of time. Alternatively, if operating from further out, NATO aircraft would need to rely on tanker refuelling. While the Alliance maintains a substantial tanker fleet, the presence of a ground and maritime IADS which can target tankers over most of northern Norway and the Barents Sea will force tanker orbits further back. This is of particular salience for the operation of aircraft such as the F-35A and F-35B from distant airfields. The aircraft, with combat radiuses of 800 and 1,000 km, respectively, would need two to three tanker orbits to conduct missions over the Kola Peninsula if operating from NATO air bases in the UK or Germany.[30] Final tanker orbits between 400–600 km of the peninsula would place these aircraft within reach of either maritime or ground-based SAM systems, as well as MIG-31BM interceptors. If, on the other hand, orbits are further out, this will limit the time an aircraft can spend on station.

Carrier-enabled power projection can partially alleviate this challenge – insofar as aircraft launched from carriers in the Norwegian Sea would need fewer tanker refuelling orbits to reach their targets. As described in the chapter on ASuW, aircraft carriers are reasonably survivable against long-range strike assets like the Kinzhal given the limitations of Russia's reconnaissance strike complex. However, the longer carriers remain in a theatre, the poorer their odds become in these interactions, as the probability of the anti-access forces completing their kill chain successfully rises with time. Moreover, given the inherent susceptibility of aircraft carriers to a single catastrophic mission kill should a munition such as the Kinzhal be targeted effectively, carrier-

---

[30] On the F-35, see Marcus Hellyer, 'Projecting Power With the F-35: How Far Will it Go?', Australian Strategic Policy Institute, 27 September 2019, <https://www.aspistrategist.org.au/projecting-power-with-the-f-35-part-1-how-far-can-it-go/>, accessed 2 May 2021.

enabled power projection is arguably more useful for raiding than longer missions such as SEAD. This having been said, a raid could be launched to eliminate the vessels that form Russia's maritime IADS and serve as launchers for land attack missiles. This could in turn serve to enable tanker refuelling. In tandem with the use of submarine-launched missiles to target assets such as the MIG-31 on the ground, such raids can serve as an enabler for follow-on sorties. This would still leave the ground-based component of Russia's IADS functional to limit the freedom of action of NATO air forces until they are eliminated.

Eliminating Russian SAM systems is likely to be a difficult task for two reasons. First, with the exception of fifth-generation fighters, most NATO aircraft will likely face significant risks when attempting to suppress an IADS and will need to rely on resource-intensive enabling tasks such as cyber attacks and electronic jamming by dedicated aircraft such as the US Navy's EA-18G. Jamming, for example, requires detailed signals analysis to identify emissions and cyber attacks require time-intensive efforts to infiltrate an adversary system well in advance of a conflict. Moreover, the effects of both type of attack are temporary.[31] As such, it is reasonable to assume a high level of attrition for anything other than fifth-generation aircraft over the Kola Peninsula.

Moreover, it is reasonable to assume that even fifth-generation aircraft are not invulnerable. During the 1980s, US Air Force planners assumed an attrition rate of 1.5% per sortie for fourth-generation aircraft operating against the Russian SAM systems of the day.[32] While the stealth of fifth-generation aircraft does represent a technological step change, defensive systems have evolved significantly since the 1980s as well. Even assuming that the offense-defence balance – at least with regard to fifth-generation aircraft – has moved radically in favour of the attacker, sortie attrition rates of 0.5% would still produce cumulative losses. Historical evidence from the 20th century suggests, moreover, that air attrition against a credible IADS, even in the face of a power and technology mismatch, tends to be in the range of 1–5%.[33] Given the limited number of available fifth-generation aircraft, this is not trivial.

---

[31] Bronk, 'Russian and Chinese IADS', p. 28.

[32] Posen, *Inadvertent Escalation,* p. 200.

[33] Based on attrition rates from the Yom Kippur War, Vietnam War and Second World War. See Guenter Lewy, *America in Vietnam* (New York, NY: Oxford University Press, 1978); Historical Evaluation and Research Service, *The Development of Soviet Air Defence Doctrine and Practice* (Dunn Loring, VA: T. N. Dupuy Associates, 1981), pp. 30–35; Posen, *Inadvertent Escalation,* p. 220.

Even if aircraft survive, this does not necessarily mean they will accomplish their mission. A layered defence such as that deployed on the Kola Peninsula has the potential to significantly thin the herd of strike munitions, even if aircraft launching munitions evade detection. On the one hand, low observable low-flying munitions can pose challenges to air defenders. However, Russian air defences have largely optimised against this challenge. The 76N6 and 30N6E can be mast mounted, extending their horizons against low-flying targets to 40 km.[34] Moreover, networking ground-based systems with MIG-31BMs would also significantly increase their ability to track low-flying objects – as will the presence of Resonans and Sopka radar (though these systems will contribute to alertness rather than tracking per se). Modelling conducted in this area tends to assume a Pk of 0.8–0.9 for modern air-defence systems against long-range cruise missiles should targeting cycles enable a 'shoot-look-shoot' doctrine – though low-flying missiles with a small RCS and emerging hypersonic prompt strike capabilities can shift this balance.[35] Shorter-range interceptors such as the 9V55 and the 9M96E/E2 as well as point defence systems, such as the Pantsir, can provide an effective defence against the munitions that NATO aircraft are likely to carry. This raises the size of the sortie necessary to initiate successful attacks. Also, SAM operators can operate based on 'shoot-and-scoot' tactics – something for which the S-300PMU and S-400 are optimised. Furthermore, decoy camouflage and other forms of operational deception will be employed by skilled operators. Historical evidence from the Kosovo conflict, in which Serbian air defenders proved adept at camouflage and movement, suggests that SEAD is likely to be partial under these conditions – NATO eliminated only three out of 25 Serbian batteries.[36]

Finally, the air operating environment will be impacted by strategic EW systems like the Murmansk-BN, based out of the EW centre at Severomorsk. It can suppress high-frequency communication over

[34] Michael Kofman, 'Russian A2/AD: It Is Not Overrated, Just Poorly Understood', Russian Military Analysis blog, <https://russianmilitaryanalysis.wordpress.com/2020/01/25/russian-a2-ad-it-is-not-overrated-just-poorly-understood/>, accessed 10 May 2021.
[35] For examples of this modelling for Russian and US systems, see Michael Pelosi and Amy Honeycutt, 'Cruise Missile Integrated Air Defence System Penetration: Modelling the S-400', *International Journal of Aviation, Aeronautics and Aerospace* (Vol. 4, No. 3), pp. 1–24; Thomas Shugart and Javier Gonzales, *First Strike: The Chinese Missile Threat to US Bases in East Asia* (Washington, DC: CNAS, 2018,) p. 12.
[36] Christopher Blockom, *Military Suppression of Enemy Air Defences: Assessing Future Needs* (Washington, DC: Congressional Research Service, 2005), p. 6.

ranges of up to 540 nm.[37] As such, the ability of aircraft to share and receive information over datalinks will be at least partially compromised, with implications for force coordination. It is also worth noting that the Severodvinsk EW centre's other systems, such as the Krashuka, will contribute to point defence against air-launched munitions by targeting their guidance systems. This is not to say that the region will be an information denied environment for NATO – improvements in areas such as satellite communications can partially offset the effects of EW.[38] However, the importance of high frequency communications to most NATO systems and to networks such as link 16 will make neutralising Russian EW capabilities a major objective for NATO assets.

As such, in the early stages of any conflict, NATO would struggle to maintain the sortie rates over the Kola Peninsula needed to prosecute SEAD and OCA missions. Moreover, the suppression of the IADS system on the peninsula would likely be time and resource consuming, and it would involve a significant level of attrition of both aircraft and munitions. The combination of layered hard and soft kill measures erected by Russia on the peninsula suggests that, at least in this part of the Arctic, Russia has met its aspiration of being able to deflect the effects of Western air advantages.

On the other hand, in the central and eastern portions of the Arctic, a different picture emerges. The relative paucity of SAM systems in these areas means that they are very thinly defended. Of course, SAM batteries can be surged to the region, but the number of AN-124 aircraft available for this task is limited to only nine – meaning that the movement of strategic SAM systems at pace may prove difficult. Moreover, the relatively limited number of MIG-31 interceptors needed to cover this area represent a point of fragility which can be targeted on the ground with SLCMs – an approach rendered all the more viable by Russia's defensive disadvantages in the subsurface domain. There is, then, a real possibility that this northern flank can be turned using submarine-launched prompt strike capabilities and strategic bombers. American air operations from Alaska represent another risk. The early-warning radar coverage provided by the Sopka-2 radar on Kotelny and Wrangel, coupled with the ability of the MIG-31BM to act as a cruise missile

---

[37] Thomas Withington, 'Offence for Defence?', Armada International, 7 July 2021, <https://armadainternational.com/2021/01/offence-for-defence/>, accessed 21 December 2021.

[38] See, for example, Nathan Strout, 'How 2 Space Norway Satellites Will Help the Air Force in the Arctic', C4ISRNet, <https://www.c4isrnet.com/battlefield-tech/2019/07/05/how-2-space-norway-satellites-will-help-the-air-force-in-the-arctic/>, accessed 21 December 2021.

interceptor, can presumably partially mitigate the first threat. However, the operation of strategic bombers against the critical infrastructure of Russia's High North appears to be an asymmetrical vulnerability that Russia is yet to offset. As such, in the Central and Eastern Arctic – regions of critical economic importance – Russia has significant vulnerabilities.

CHAPTER V: RUSSIAN LAND AND AMPHIBIOUS CAPABILITIES IN THE ARCTIC

Key Points

- Russia's ground forces in the region are comparatively modest, but they can contribute to sub-threshold competition in a meaningful way.
- The ability to surge assets to the region, and the Arctic training of the air force, could see this force grow rapidly in wartime.
- Limitations on Russia's airlift and sealift capabilities still represent a major constraint on operations in the High North.
- Despite this, Russia will enjoy relative advantages on the ground over most of the Arctic due to its geographical proximity and infrastructure investments.

The maritime nature of the theatre has seen the prominence of air and naval power in Russia's Arctic build-up. Nonetheless, Russia does have an increasingly credible, though still limited, suite of rapidly deployable ground and amphibious capabilities in the region. Large portions of the Russian force structure not held within Russia's Arctic-facing commands, including the air force, have been practising regional missions since 2014 and, as air-mobile forces, could likely be rapidly deployed there. NATO forces are also permanently present in the High North – built around the Norwegian army's Brigade Nord – but are limited. However, Norway is likely to be reinforced in a conflict. Frameworks such as the UK-led Joint Expeditionary Force might be mobilised in a crisis scenario, with the Royal Marines having a major role in High North operations. Exercises such as *Trident Juncture* and Amphibious Leaders Expeditionary Symposium wargames also suggest European rapid reaction forces flowing into Norway as part of a US-led Marine Expeditionary Unit. The modelling from previous chapters suggests that in wartime, Russian anti-access capabilities could slow this flow of forces if they are not attritted.

However, should there be a Russian build-up during a crisis, this would likely provide NATO with warning sufficient to commence the movement of elements of the VJTF, as well as national rapid-reaction forces, into theatre. Those Russian assets that are in the region, by contrast, are geared towards defence and could carry out only limited offensive operations.

Russia's ground forces in the Arctic are under the 14th Army Corps, itself subordinate to the Northern Fleet's Joint Strategic Command. The 14th Corps can provide C2 to both ground and coastal defence units and is comprised of two mechanised brigades – the 210th and the 80th.[1] The Coastal Defence Forces of the fleet also include the units of the 61st Naval Infantry brigade. Coastal defence units such as the 536th Coastal Missile and Artillery Brigade equipped with Bal and Bastion-P batteries are also under the Command's Coastal Defence Forces.[2] While not comparable in size or equipment to the units held within Russia's other military districts, this force appears to demonstrate both an increasing degree of specialisation for its Arctic function and an ability to generate flexible units such as the 99th tactical group and the separate missile air defence and infantry formations on Alexandra Land, which are tailored to the needs of persistent competition in the High North. The protection against infiltration by amphibious forces of 'enclaves' in remote areas defended by air defence and coastal missile batteries has been made a primary function of the naval infantry, which may well find itself spread across islands in the region supporting tactical groups.[3] The construction of tri-service facilities will allow these units to maintain a regional presence that other states may find difficult to match.

The Russian armed forces have a significant, though declining, capability to move forces both into and around the region. Russia maintains a robust strategic airlift capability, though the number of aircraft available has declined significantly over the past few years, partially due to the closure of access to suppliers such as Antonov in Ukraine.[4] The Northern Fleet also has a limited amphibious capability,

---

[1] Lester Grau and Charles Bartles, *The Russian Way of War* (Fort Leavenworth, KS: Foreign Military Studies Office, 2016), p. 30.
[2] Grau and Bartles, *The Russian Way of War*; David Batashvili, 'Russian Military Forces: Interactive Map', Rondeli Foundation, first published 7 August 2018, <https://www.gfsis.org/maps/view/russian-military-forces>, accessed 10 May 2021.
[3] Charles Bartles, 'Change Is Coming for Russian Naval Infantry Brigades', Foreign Military Studies Office, 1 January 2020, <https://community.apan.org/wg/tradoc-g2/fmso/m/oe-watch-articles-2-singular-format/348896>, accessed 20 November 2021.
[4] Anastasia Dagaeva, 'Antonov: The Unsung Victim of the Russia–Ukraine Conflict', Carnigie Moscow Center, <https://carnegie.ru/commentary/75944>, accessed 14 November 2021.

based on the *Ropucha*-and *Ivan Gren*-class landing ships, which would likely be augmented with civilian vessels to support troop movement. While insufficient to mount opposed theatre entry, these assets can move and resupply Russian forces along the NSR, enabling rapid redeployment. The *Ropucha*-class demonstrated this during the Syrian conflict where the Black Sea Fleet's limited number were critical to resupplying Russian forces in Syria.[5]

Primarily, then, the force structure that Russia has developed on the ground in the Arctic appears well suited to move tailored, rapidly deployable formations around the region at short notice. This can support purely defensive functions of offshore islands or far-flung regions of the Russian Arctic.[6] In principle, these forces could also support the Russian navy in sea control functions – for example, by aiding maritime interdiction and boarding. This force could – in tandem with external support from other military districts – act as a spearhead for limited offensive activities in a conflict. For example, Russia could attempt to neutralise airfields in Northern Norway, long assumed to be a part of Soviet Cold War planning or pursue a strategic feint to draw NATO assets from another front.[7]

This chapter will argue that Russia's Arctic ground forces will support only limited competitive objectives, and will be hampered by a number of factors should their ambitions extend beyond this. It is worth flagging that this chapter primarily considers the assets of OSK Sever – which are tasked with Arctic security – but also considers the potential role of ground assets from other military districts.

Russian Ground Forces in the Arctic: Force Structure and Equipment

The Arctic Brigade, formed under the Northern Fleet Joint Strategic Command, is generated from two parent units, the 200th Independent Motor Rifle Brigade and the 80th Mechanized Arctic Brigade, which are based at Pechenga and Alakurtti, respectively. The two motor rifle brigades' orders of battle and equipment are as follows:[8]

---

[5] H I Sutton, 'The Russian Navy's Relay Resupplying Syria Continues', *Naval News*, 24 March 2020, <https://www.navalnews.com/naval-news/2020/03/the-russian-navys-bosphorus-relay-resupplying-syria-continues/>, accessed 21 December 2021.

[6] Boulègue, *Russia's Military Posture in the Arctic*. While this sort of attack by NATO may be unlikely, similar potential actions were planned during the Cold War as forms of horizontal escalation to offset Soviet strengths in Central Europe, see Mearsheimer, 'A Strategic Misstep'.

[7] Posen, *Inadvertent Escalation*, pp. 50–60.

[8] Batashvili, 'Russian Military'; Boulègue, *Russia's Military Posture in the Arctic*.

200th Independent Motor Rifle Brigade

ORBAT

Three mechanised battalions
One tank battalion
One recon battalion
One sniper company
One UAV company
Two self-propelled howitzer battalions
One reactive artillery battalion
One anti-tank artillery battalion
Two air-defence battalions

Equipment

40+ tanks
About 170 armoured personnel carriers
36 self-propelled howitzers
18 multiple-rocket launchers
18 mortars
12 self-propelled anti-tank missile systems
12 anti-tank guns

80th Mechanized Arctic Brigade

ORBAT

Three mechanised battalions
One recon battalion
One sniper company
One UAV company
One self-propelled howitzer battalion
One air-defence battalion

Equipment

Military unit number: 34,667
150+ armoured personnel carriers
Unknown number of cross-country vehicles and multi-purpose articulated tracked carriers
18 self-propelled howitzers: 122-mm Gvodzika, 20 km range
18 mortars
In addition, the Russian naval infantry's 61st Brigade is located near Sputnik Air Base, with the following ORBAT and capabilities.[9]

---

[9] *BMPD Journal,* 'Modernizirovannyye tanki T-80BV morskoy pekhoty Severnogo flota' ['Modernised T-80BV Tanks of the Northern Fleet Marine Corps'], March 2018,

61st Naval Infantry Brigade
ORBAT

Two naval infantry battalions
One assault battalion
One tank company
One recon company
One flamethrower company
Two self-propelled artillery battalions
One reactive battery
One anti-tank battery
One air defence battalion

Equipment

130+ armoured personnel carriers
10 tanks
12 self-propelled howitzers
22 self-propelled guns
Six multiple rocket launchers

Russia's Arctic ground forces will likely be supported in many operations by attack aviation. The 98th Separate Mixed Aviation Regiment based in Monchegorsk has MI-24 attack helicopters. The 830th Independent Helicopter regiment operating from Severomorsk-1 has the Ka-29.

This force structure is significant, although not formidable and this force brings to bear far more limited long-range fire capability than in other districts. There are only a limited number of MLRS systems allocated to the region, for example. Similarly, the amount of armour in the force is limited to around four companies, three of which are part of the 200th Brigade. However, two characteristics of this force are worth noting – its specialisation and the integration of capabilities within the force.

Both the naval infantry and the 200th Motor Rifle have received Arctic-specialised assets that will significantly improve their ability to operate in the region's conditions. Both units have been equipped with the T-80BVM which, with its gas turbine engine, can allegedly operate more effectively in the region than diesel-powered tanks.[10] The 200th and 80th

---

<https://bmpd.livejournal.com/3187758.html>, accessed 21 December 2021; Batashvili, 'Russian Military Forces'.

[10] *WeaponSystem.net*, 'T-80BVM', <https://weaponsystems.net/system/835-T-80BVM>, accessed 1 May 2021; there is some disagreement on the suitability of the vehicle for the Arctic, see Alex Tarasoff, 'T-80BVM Flatters to Deceive as an Arctic Tank', *Shephard*, 15 April 2021.

regiments have also received the MT-LBV armoured personnel carrier, which is more mobile in Arctic conditions due to its having wider tracks than the original MT-LB, the TTM-1901 Berkut snowmobile, adapted to regional conditions and the amphibious-capable GAZ-3344-20 personnel carrier.[11] The short-range air defence capabilities of Russia's Arctic units, such as the Pantsir-SA, are also built with Arctic-specific characteristics such as the DT-30 all-terrain chassis.[12]

The second feature of the ground-force structure in the Arctic is its integration and flexibility. Formations such as the 99th Arctic tactical group, which combine coastal defence systems from the 536th, Pantsir batteries and limited numbers of infantry, illustrate the ability of the Arctic Brigade to generate unique self-sustaining formations for tasks such as localised sea control around specific features. The self-contained formation, which pulls together units from across the ground-based components of the force, represents a model where a presence can be maintained on islands. Russia's bases in areas such as Kotelny and Alexandra Land also allow for a year-round presence in these areas.

Operational and Strategic Mobility

Russia would likely attempt to surge forces to the High North in a conflict. The 76th Guards Air Assault Division and the 98th Guards Airborne Division are earmarked for missions on the Kola Peninsula. Both have been practising Arctic-specific missions and exercises since at least 2014 on regional islands.[13]

Russia maintains a significant airlift capability, though this has been in a relative decline over the past several decades. In 2017, Russia had 111 aircraft capable of supporting military airlift.[14] Of these, nine were AN-124s, which would be needed for the movement of particularly heavy assets, such as armour or additional strategic SAMs, to the Arctic.[15] The bulk of the fleet, however, is comprised of the IL-76. While the fleet has grown somewhat since, its capacity for strategic airlift has not increased significantly.[16]

Russia maintains a number of airfields in the Arctic capable of hosting strategic aircraft, including Nagurskoye and Temp on Alexandra Land and

---

[11] Boulègue, *Russia's Military Posture in the Arctic*.
[12] *WeaponSystem.net*, 'Pantsir-SA', <https://weaponsystems.net/system/151-Pantsir-SA>, accessed 14 November 2021.
[13] Boulègue, *Russia's Military Posture in the Arctic*.
[14] Tom Waldwyn, 'Russian Military Lift Risks Atrophy', IISS Military Balance Blog, 6 July 2017.
[15] Joseph Trevithick, 'Russia Is Extending One of the Runways at its Syrian Airbase', *The Drive*, 5 February 2021.
[16] Anton Lavrov, 'Russian Military Reforms from Georgia to Syria', Center for Strategic and International Studies, p. 35.

Figure 21: Trefoil Bases at Alexandra Land and Kotelny, with Shelters for Bastion-P TELS

Source: Maxar Technologies and authors'

Kotelny, respectively. However, only some of these have runways long enough to allow an AN-124 to take off or land.

Air Bases With Runways of (>3 km) Capable of Hosting AN-124

Base	Latitude, Longitude
Sredny Ostrov Air Base	91,07579,528334
Anadyr Ugolny Airport	77,7564,720913,64
Olenya Air Base	33,4768,151673,56A
Nagurskoye Air Base	47,4797280,798613,5A
Sovetskiy Air Base	64,3077867,465563,48A
Lakhta Naval Air Base	40,7166764,383333,1A
Aeroport Tiksi	128,902871,69753,06A
Pechora – Airfield	56,6733365,0553

Air Base With Runways (<3 km, >2.5 km)

Base	Latitude, Longitude
Norilks Dual-Use Airport	87,3435369,325412,85
Amderma Airport	61,5784969,759512,56
Provideniya Bay Airport-	173,24364,378332,54
Naryan-Mar Air Base	53,12567,642,53
Airfield	32,4045269,096232,51
Mys Shmidta Airport	179,37668,868332,5

Air Bases Capable of Hosting IL-76

Base	Latitude, Longitude
Rogachevo Military Base	52,4675471,611992,43
Severomorsk-3 Air Base	33,7166768,866672,4
Monchegorsk Air Base	33,0307667,989922,39
Vorkuta Dual Use Airport	64,0094467,491062,18
Alakurtti Air Base	30, 34566,973332,17
Temp Air Base – Kotelny	137,741775,766672,1
Luostari Pechenga Air Base	30,9883369,41,73

In terms of sealift, Russia maintains an amphibious fleet comprised of seven *Ropucha* landing ships, as well as one active *Ivan Gren*.[17] The *Ivan Gren* were purchased to replace the Mistrals which Russia had ordered from France. However, the sale was suspended because of the 2014 Crimea invasion, and the Russian-made vessels are not comparable to the Mistral. They are smaller than Western landing ships, such as the *Albion*, and have the capacity to carry 300 troops or 13 main battle tanks.[18] The *Ropucha* proved their worth as transport vessels during Russian operations in Syria, in which the vessels took part alongside the larger Project 1171. Although they lack the well deck and C2 suite of the *Ivan Gren*, the vessels do have a greater lift capacity. The vessels are built to carry two companies of naval infantry and can also ferry up to 13 MBTs.[19]

While this force cannot conduct opposed landings at scale, it can probably move mixed tactical groups between islands across the Arctic. They can also resupply units on island outposts, in tandem with airlift capabilities. The Russian ground forces in the region have a meaningful but still limited degree of intra-theatre mobility.

The Capabilities of Russian Ground Assets in the Arctic

It appears, then, that Russia's organic ground capabilities in the Arctic are limited. However, Russian forces in the region do appear capable of supporting a range of competitive activities along the NSR. For example,

---

[17] RussianShips.info, <http://russianships.info/eng/warships/project_775.htm>, accessed 10 May 2021.

[18] Naval Technology, 'Project 11711 Ivan Gren Class Landing Ships', <https://www.naval-technology.com/projects/project-11711-ivan-gren-class-landing-ships/>, accessed 10 May 2021.

[19] GlobalSecurity.org, 'Project 775 Ropucha Class Tank Landing Ship', <https://www.globalsecurity.org/military/world/russia/775.htm'>, accessed 10 May 2021; on the Syrian resupply operation, see Foreign Military Studies Office, 'Russian Military Expeditionary Capability: A Relatively Low Priority', <https://community.apan.org/wg/tradoc-g2/fmso/w/o-e-watch-mobile-edition-v1/22721/russian-expeditionary-capabilities-a-relatively-low-priority/>, accessed 10 May 2021.

Russia's 99th Arctic tactical group represents a viable formation for aiding sea control missions along the route. The exercising of Arctic Brigade, naval infantry and air force units on both land and sea raises the possibility that these could be used for policing, such as maritime interdiction in peacetime that could take on a competitive hue. The robust infrastructure of Russia's trefoil bases could allow these units to maintain a persistent presence along the NSR, resupplied by both air- and sealift.

In a conflict scenario, Russian ground forces in the Arctic have limited offensive options. Although they do outgun their Norwegian counterparts and could conduct limited offensives to seize territory as a bargaining chip, their ability to hold ground will depend on Russia's ability to back up and resupply a northern spearhead force.

CONCLUSIONS

At the outset of this paper, the authors set out to present the current balance of power in the Arctic region. The paper was structured to achieve two subordinate objectives: assess the present Russia-NATO balance of power in the Arctic; and analyse the level of ambition that Russian investment in the region can support.

A key finding that emerges from the research is the degree to which the Arctic is a region in which a balance of power exists, but is heavily tilted towards offence. In particular, the weaknesses of both sides over the defensive components of subsurface warfare render aggressive submarine activity an increasingly appealing option for NATO. This dynamic extends to the surface, however, with NATO paying a heavier price for maintaining a reactive posture than adopting a forward maritime posture.

The regional balance of power is also based on temporal and geographical factors. In the Western Arctic and the High North, where the bulk of Russia's military and economic interests lie, it appears to have effective escalation dominance. On the ground, in the air and, in many cases, at sea, Russian forces can achieve a dominant position, at least in the early stages of a conflict. The ability of Russian submarines to penetrate NATO barriers will make the reinforcement of the High North difficult, should conflict erupt there. If NATO has sufficient warning times to build up to the force levels seen during Exercise *Trident Juncture* and demanded by the NRI, by contrast, the balance of power is more contested, the Alliance enjoying offensive advantages but struggling when Russian forces take the operational initiative.

Russia's position in the central and eastern parts of the Arctic is more tenuous. While it can exert a significant level of influence over the NSR, Russia's air-defence network here is less dense than on the Kola Peninsula. This could be crucial should NATO choose to escalate horizontally using US strategic bombers. In the eastern parts of the Arctic, a relatively thin Russian air and sea defence network would be vulnerable to operations from Alaska. In both cases, this might incentivise early pre-emptive Russian action against airfields using sea-based precision strike capabilities. Indeed, targeting airfields in Greenland has already been signposted as a priority in Russian planning.

In circumstances short of high-intensity conflict, Russia enjoys a much more uncontested level of control. Its fleet of civilian icebreakers and substantial military investment along the NSR mean that it enjoys effective escalation dominance across the High North in any such circumstance. Russia enjoys a number of early advantages if it initiates a conflict before NATO mobilises. This includes holding NATO airpower at bay and the ability to penetrate the Alliance's ASW barriers. This potentially opens the way for operations, including deep strikes, SLOC interdiction and, in the case of GUGI submarines, sabotage. However, Russia also faces challenges which can be exploited by a forward-postured military approach should the Alliance opt for one.

For the Western Alliance, then, this presents both challenges and opportunities. The relative vulnerability of an area that will likely become ever-more crucial to Russia's economic security and military force posture could allow the Alliance to explore options for horizontal escalation that offset Russia's advantages on the ground in theatres like the Baltics. This being said, the escalatory potential of these options will need to be weighed. The challenge for Western powers is that passive containment – the approach taken during the Cold War – is likely to not be an option in light of the mutually offence-dominated operating environment.

In circumstances short of all-out war, Russia enjoys a number of advantages due to its local peacetime military preponderance as well as its advantages in critical civilian assets such as icebreakers. The combination of the civilian capabilities needed to support international shipping and the coercive capacity to hinder it – backed by Russia's local military preponderance in peacetime – makes Russia's efforts to exert administrative control over the NSR highly viable. This would allow Russia to exert a level of peacetime control over what might become an important maritime artery and reinforce its strategic position in competition with NATO. This is a crucial weakness for the Alliance if it is more likely to be engaged in low-intensity competition along the Northern Sea Route than in high-intensity combat.

The emerging balance of power in the High North and Arctic, then, ought to be a key concern for NATO, which will need to consider how to both reinforce its peacetime posture and how to leverage its military opportunities in wartime without provoking undesirable escalation. The questions of how members of the Alliance can leverage both its civilian and military capabilities to exert a more persistent presence in the region, as well as how the deterrent potential of NATO's options for horizontal escalation can be leveraged, should be the subject of subsequent research.

Afterword

This Whitehall Paper was written before the Russian invasion of Ukraine on 24 February 2022. Thus, some of the units discussed may no longer be in their peacetime locations. Nonetheless, the conflict does not alter our core conclusions.

APPENDIX 1: SALVO COMBAT
MODELS FOR SURFACE WARFARE

The modelling conducted to examine the balance of power in ASuW is laid out in brief here. This appendix will be of use for readers attempting to replicate the authors' findings or to test hypotheses with their own input data. The logic of modelling a single salvo exchange is described below. The campaign analysis allowed each party a set number of salvos depending on information advantage – NATO secures the first salvo in an offensive posture, for example. These assumptions depend on the authors' qualitative analysis and are exogenous to the model, which can be tested with different assumptions.

To examine the balance of power on the ocean surface, the authors used two stylised salvo combat models derived from the work of Wayne Hughes. The first model examines the risk to assets at the GIUK Gap posed by long-range strike assets, such as the Backfire bomber and the MIG-31K, as well as SSGN-launched P-800 Oniks missiles. The second examines an engagement closer to the Russian bastion in which a NATO CSG backed by two surface action groups – 13 vessels in all – confronts the surface forces of the Northern Fleet. The latter model is useful for examining whether NATO can support missions such as SEAD against the Kola Peninsula using carrier-enabled power projection. Sorties by NATO airborne strike assets are treated as part of its salvos, with munitions loads multiplied by sortie rates. This is consistent with previous work on battles in the Pacific theatre in which airborne sorties were incorporated into the salvo combat model.

For the first model, the authors assume that Russian OTH targeting can provide the location of any given vessel with an uncertainty of 20 km. Based on this, Russian combat aviation and MPAs can conduct sorties to provide more granular data or Russian anti-access capabilities can be 'fired blind' to saturate the area of uncertainty.

The lethality of Russian forces under conditions of information advantage, such as when they have granular targeting information, can be calculated using two adaptations of Hughes's original models, an aimed fire and an area fire model. The area fire model assumes that an attacker has a rough understanding of its target's location, but must rely on the organic capabilities of its missiles – the seekers on cruise missiles, for example – to search the area for a target. By contrast, the aimed fire model assumes that a missile is being fired at a target with a known location and bearing.

According to the area fire model, the ratio within which a target may be relative to the sweepwidth of a missile is given by m. The sweepwidth of a missile may vary – cruise missiles, for example, should have a sweepwidth of 5 km² while anti-ship ballistic missiles have a radius of 20 km.[1] For modelling purposes, given the heterogeneity of the missiles Russia can use from the Kinzhal to the KH-22 and 32, the authors vary the value of m between 0.03 and 0.5. Assuming assets such as the Kinzhal are scarce, the latter value is used in most of the runs to simulate cruise missile area fire.

The Pk against a single warship is, then, given by

$$Pk = (A.mB - ZB)u$$

Where A is the number of offensive missiles fired, ZB is the probability of kill of the blue forces defensive firepower times the number of interceptors available and u is the staying power of a given ship.

For aimed fire, the figure is derived through

$$(A - Zb)u$$

For modelling purposes, the single shot Pk of defensive interceptors is assumed to be between 0.6 and 0.8, which is an optimistic assumption for defenders but is consistent with previous work on air and missile defence.[2] Given the asymmetry in speed between Russian and NATO missiles, however, the Pk of NATO IAMD is likely to be closer to 0.6, if not lower. This represents a necessary simplification.

To model a surface contest closer to the bastion, the authors used Michael Armstrong's stochastic salvo model. The model represents an evolution of Hughes's work but incorporates a degree of variation, making it amenable to being used in Monte Carlo simulations.[3]

---

[1] Eric Hagt and Matthew Durnin, 'Chinese Antiship Ballistic Missile – Developments and Missing Links', *Naval War College Review* (Volume 62, No. 4, 2009), 1–31, p. 9.

[2] Thomas Shugart, *First Strike: China's Missile Threat to US Bases in Asia* (Washington, DC: CNAS, 2017), p. 15.

[3] For details, see Michael Armstrong, 'A Stochastic Salvo Model for Naval Surface Combat', *Operations Research* (Vol. 53, No. 5, Sept–Oct 2005), pp. 830–41.

The number of well-targeted rounds fired by each side in this context (henceforth referred to as R and N-Russia and NATO) is given as

$$A = A\sigma_a^2$$

If each round has a probability Pa of successful launch, determined on the basis of each side's sensor coverage as well as the target's use of decoys and other electronic countermeasures, the variance is given by $\sigma = A.Pa.(1-pa)$. The inclusion of a standard distribution allows for the consideration of the effects of ISR failures, adversary soft kill and guidance system failures. In order to assess the defensive capabilities of each fleet, a similar process is undertaken for B (the intercept probability). The surviving number of ships after a given salvo is given by

$$B - (A - ZB)u$$

And the variance is given by

$$(A - ZB)\sigma_u^2 + (A\sigma_a^2 + B\sigma_z^2) + 2\sigma_u^2(\sigma_u^2 + B\sigma_z^2)u^2\,G(o)$$
$$- 2\sigma_u^2(A\sigma_a^2 - ZB\sigma_z^2)g(0)$$

Where g and G represent the probability distribution and cumulative distribution functions and the distribution is assumed to be normal.

The actual losses for B need to account for the fact that the number of incoming missiles is an integer that is being modelled as a cumulative distribution. Thus a continuity correction of U/2 is introduced.

The actual mean losses of B is given by

$$\int_{0+u/2}^{B-u/2} tg_b t(dt) + G_b\left(B - \frac{u}{2}\right)$$

And the variance by

$$\int_{0+u/2}^{B-u/2} t^2 g_b t(dt) + B^2\left(1 - G_b\left(B - \frac{u}{2}\right) - E(Bs)\right)^2$$

With E(Bs) representing the average value of surviving vessels at any given time.

Both these values can be expressed in terms of the nominal losses and variance for incorporation into a spreadsheet.

Two factors now need to be considered: the inclusion of ground-based systems; and air-based systems. For the purposes of the model, these systems were incorporated as effectively invulnerable shooters. Their missile and organic radar search capabilities were added to the values of Russian salvos without a corresponding platform. This is a good approximation of reality insofar as the suppression of both types of shooter will be difficult due to their range (in the case of bombers), stealth (for fifth-generation aircraft) and 'shoot-and-scoot' capabilities (in the case of ground-based TELS) and the fact that they operate within a protective IADS. However, this is still a major limitation of the authors' modelling process, which subsequent research can potentially rectify.

APPENDIX 2: SUBMARINE ASW INTERACTIONS

The detection of submarines by ASW capabilities including MPAs, frigates and SSNs is a function of two factors:

- The likelihood that a submarine can exploit a gap in the ASW barrier.
- The ability of ASW assets, upon detection, to mitigate uncertainty about the submarine's location to enable tracking and subsequent engagement.

To model the first factor, Washburn's barrier was used as a search model. According to this model, an asset at a barrier against an intruder travels at speed U and executes a path optimised to cover as much of its sector as possible in a single circuit, while minimising wasteful coverage outside the search area. This is an idealisation, and not entirely representative of reality.

Assuming a target, such as a submarine, is moving towards the barrier at velocity V, the relative motion of the searcher and evader is given by

$$S = \sqrt{U^2 + V^2 - 2UV(Cos(y))}$$

Where Cos Y is the angle between the two objects velocity vectors, which averages to 0 in a search pattern that is a closed curve.

The probability of detection of an individual searcher against an individual evader is

$$\frac{2RS}{UL}$$

Where R is the cookie-cutter detection radius of the searcher's sensor and L is the length of the portion of the barrier that it is patrolling.

This model, while a useful starting point, is crude in a number of ways, most notably:

- An inability to incorporate sensor inaccuracy.
- An inability to incorporate network effects as ASW platforms coordinate.
- The relative absence of stochasticity in key variables.

It has therefore been used as a baseline for a more complete representation of the hider/seeker dynamics involved.

First, sensor uncertainty is incorporated into the authors' framework in two ways.

they account for the effects of factors such as Bathymetry wind and surface noise to create uncertainty.

The baseline equation on which detection is modelled is

$$TL = SL - NL + AG - DT$$

Where TL is transmission loss, SL is source noise level at 1m, NL is the ambient noise level and DT is the detection threshold.

The authors' follow Eugene Miasnikov in assuming an array gain of 12 db at a frequency of 50 hz for a towed-array sonar, and 7 db for a hull-mounted one.

The detection threshold of a submarine is dependent on the detection index, which is determined by probability density functions of the signal amplitude to the signal plus noise amplitude. The detection index is given by

$$\frac{(S+N) - N)\hat{2}}{\sigma\hat{2}}$$

Where (S+N) is the average amplitude of the signal plus noise and N is the amplitude of background noise and variance is assumed to be gaussian.

A detection index value of 21 corresponding to a (probably optimistic) detection probability of 0.8 and a probability of false alarm of 10^{-4} is assumed for this paper.

The detection threshold can then be derived through

$$5 log_{10}\left(\frac{dW}{t}\right)$$

Where W is the bandwidth of the receiver and t is the integration time. It is assumed that narrowband processing is preferred against quiet submarines, implying a bandwidth of 10–100 hz. Beyond 100 hz the tonals of newer submarines are not detectable. Integration time is assumed to be 100 seconds, for which the authors have no data but which amounts to a relatively optimistic assumption for the seeker.[1] This yields a DT of 6.93 at 50 hz.

Ambient noise levels in the Norwegian and Barents Seas at 50 hz are approximately 77 db for the former, and 72 db for the latter. The Arctic varies significantly, with noise levels of up to 110 db at marginal ice zones and as low as 30 db in the central Arctic.[2] Based on these assumptions, detection ranges can be deduced using the inverse square law. The authors are able to incorporate sensor inaccuracy, including pd and pfa, into their model.

Second, an attempt is made to incorporate the effect of networking by decreasing the area that needs to be searched in some trials. If a platform is cued by, for example, a sonobuoy barrier or a hydrophone network such as SOSUS, it already has a rough idea of where its target is. As such, its search radius is a function of the time it takes to reach the location and the area the submarine can have moved in this time. For example, the search radius of FFGs and MPAs is decreased in some trials, proportionate to the number of successful detections by hydrophone barriers, which narrow their search parameters and make their task easier. The authors did this by modelling a layered defensive system, in which FFGs and MPAs are held behind a line of SSNs that are themselves behind a hydrophone barrier. The detection of a submarine by a hydrophone barrier is treated as a Flemings datum point, cueing in an MPA which, in other runs, lays sonabuoys in a random search pattern across likely routes of travel. While networking assets is an aspiration in ASW, limitations on interoperability across Allied assets, adversary disruption and a host of other factors make a quasi-networked system more likely. This means that using models of ASW both with and without effective cueing is most effective. For active systems such as magnetic anomaly detectors and dipping sonar, the authors assume a cookie-cutter detection rate of 1 nm, consistent with previous work in this area.[3]

[1] National Research Council, *Technology for the United States Navy and Marine Corps, 2000–2035: Becoming a 21st-Century Force, Volume 7: Undersea Warfare* (Washington, DC: National Academies Press, 1997).
[2] Dixon and Rollins, 'Very Low Frequency Acoustic Detection of Submarines'; Grenness, 'Acoustic Ambient Noise in the Barents Sea'.
[3] Gerald Brown et al., *A Game-Theoretic Model for Defence of an Oceanic Bastion Against Submarines* (Monterey, CA: Naval Postgraduate School, 2011).

Printed in Great Britain
by Amazon

32293458R00064